PRAISE FOR DARLA NELSON

"As The Father of Afformations®, I've seen how one simple shift in thinking can change everything. In her powerful book *I'm Fine. Really?*, Darla Nelson shows what happens when that shift becomes a way of life. This book is raw, real, and filled with breakthroughs. Her story is proof that when you stop faking 'I'm fine' and start asking the right questions, healing happens. I'm honored that my Afformations® Method has helped shape not only her journey, but also the lives she's now impacting."

-Dr. Noah St. John, The Father of Afformations® and Creator of The 12-Week Breakthrough

"*I'm Fine! Really?* is a heartfelt and powerful guide for anyone feeling unseen, unheard, or overwhelmed by the burdens they carry. Through candid storytelling and spiritual insight, Darla reminds us that healing begins with honesty, with ourselves and with God. Her book is a moving call to acknowledge our pain, reclaim our purpose, and find true peace beyond the facade of 'fine.' It's a brave and beautiful testament to the strength found in surrender."

-Cassandra Augusto, publisher of Neighbors of East Turlock Magazine

"This book has the potential to profoundly transform how we think, speak, and approach life. It offers encouragement and tools to shift our mindset in ways that can positively impact our financial, emotional, and mental well-being. *I'm Fine, Really?* is a beautiful invitation to embrace personal growth and discover the power of intentional thought."

-Tammy Littlefield, How Money Works Financial Educator

"I'm Fine. Really? is more than a book, it's a wake-up call for anyone who's been trying to hold it all together. Honest reflections about trusting God's timing, opening ourselves to new perspectives, and choosing peace over control, hit home for me. The practical tools for managing worry, renewing the mind, choosing positive habits and returning to God in the quiet moments are a gift. This book reminds us that growth starts when we're willing to think differently, live intentionally, and receive support from a God who cares about every part of our story."

-Karla Gregg Irondi, Personal Growth & Courage Coach

"Darla balances practical with spiritual inspiration in her authentic storytelling to unlock both feeling and action. The incorporation of journal prompts throughout each chapter kindly holds the reader accountable for self-reflection and encourages personal growth which is so true to Darla's coaching style."

-Jamie Bone, Ed.D

"Three letters, one word WOW! I was instantly enthralled by this book and found it difficult to put down. Darla's unwavering faith, as reflected in her experiences and insights, makes this book an indispensable read for all. Its transformative potential is undeniable!"

-Laura Donna Phillips, Speaker, Trainer & Coach

"Darla does a beautiful job of integrating scripture, and practical health and wellness tips into her life story! She brings the reader along on her beautiful journey of faith, grief, hope, and healing. I especially appreciate her thoughtful journal prompts and intentionality to enrich the heart and perspective of her audience."

-Chantelle Cadirao, Certified Life Coach

I'M FINE. REALLY?
MOVING FROM STRESS AND ANXIETY TO PEACE AND CALM

DARLA NELSON

ZAMIZ PRESS

SELF-HELP / Personal Growth / Success

RELIGION / Christian Living / Personal Growth

Special discounts are available on quantity purchases by corporations, associations and others. For details, contact the author.

DO YOU HAVE A MESSAGE TO SHARE WITH THE WORLD? ARE YOU INTERESTED IN HAVING YOUR BOOK PUBLISHED? VISIT ZAMIZPRESS.COM

All rights reserved. No part of this publication may be reproduced, distributed or transmitted in any form or by any means, including photocopying, recording, or other electronic or mechanical methods, without the prior written permission of the publisher, except in the case of brief quotations embodied in critical reviews and certain other noncommercial uses permitted by copyright law.

The information in this book is not intended to replace the advice of a physician. It is for informational purposes only and any supplement, diet, or exercise program should be started under the advisement of a physician. Author and publisher are not responsible.

Copyright © 2025 by Darla Nelson

Cover concept: Mariela Nelson

Editing: Rebecca Black

Cover design: Nathaniel Dasco

I'm Fine. Really? / Darla Nelson

ISBN: 978-1-949813-45-6

To my dad, Lloyd Wirjtes—
Though you have been gone since 2013, your influence continues to shape my life. You instilled in me a deep desire to help others think more positively, embrace life with a perspective of gratitude, and focus on what truly matters. God.
More than anything, you nurtured in me a love for Scripture, and this verse became the foundation of my passion for encouraging others: "Finally, brothers and sisters, whatever is true, whatever is noble, whatever is right, whatever is pure, whatever is lovely, whatever is admirable—if anything is excellent or praiseworthy—think about such things." (Phil. 4:8 New International Version)
Thank you dad. I love you, Darla

CONTENTS

Preface xi

Chapter 1 1
I had it all planned…

Chapter 2 5
What Grief Teaches Us: Lessons in Love and Loss

Chapter 3 17
Listening to My Body: When Health and Mindset Collide

Chapter 4 39
Stress and Its Sneaky Triggers: What's Stealing Your Peace?

Chapter 5 51
The Trap of Doing: Why Peace Comes from Being

Chapter 6 65
Words That Heal, Words That Harm: Using Your Voice for Good

Chapter 7 77
Words That Heal, Words That Hurt

Chapter 8 95
Trust Over Control: The Shift That Transformed My Life

Chapter 9 107
What's in Your Backpack? Unpacking Emotional Weight

Chapter 10 119
Faith Beyond the Familiar: Seeking Truth for Yourself

Chapter 11 125
Every Chapter Matters: Embracing the Hard Times That Build Us

Chapter 12 131
When "I'm Fine" Isn't Enough: The Hidden Cost of Pretending

Chapter 13 135
"Beyond My Understanding: Discovering the Vastness of God"

Chapter 14 139
Healthy Habits: Small Steps to a Better You

Afterword	177
What's Next	181
A Note from Darla	183
Bibliography	185
Acknowledgments	187
About the Author	189

PREFACE

This book is designed to guide you toward a mindset that fosters healthy habits, empowering you to live the joyful life you've always desired—one that nourishes your mind, body, and spirit.

As you begin reading, I want to acknowledge that faith is a deeply personal journey. I respect and honor the freedom each of us have to seek meaning, peace, and purpose in our own way. Over the past two years, I've come to realize just how much joy fills my heart when I approach others with complete love and grace—regardless of our differences in viewpoints, perspectives, or experiences.

This book is written from my heart, staying true to who I am. My faith as a Christian has profoundly shaped every area of my life, and it is the foundation of my journey. Because of this, I will often reference Scripture and prayer, as they have been invaluable sources of strength, wisdom, and peace in my life.

As you come across the verses I share, I encourage you not to simply take my word for it—dig deep, explore for yourself, and discover the truths that resonate within your own heart.

More than anything, my hope is that this book will inspire you to seek out the wisdom of Scripture and experience the lasting peace that comes from focusing on what truly matters.

MY STORY

I can't tell you when I realized I wanted to write a book.

Maybe I should just start writing and tell you a little bit about what led to the idea swirling around in my head and why I wanted to put it down on paper.

It was 2013 and my dad was experiencing heart failure. For many years he had had multiple bypasses and stents and now here we were with his health seriously declining. Other organs were beginning to be affected, and I noticed that he was realizing that maybe his time on this earth was ending.

The prior year, my parents' home had burned down due to an electrical fire and this, looking back on it, became a blessing to my husband and myself.

I believe that this fire and the stress from it were instrumental in making my dad's health decline more rapidly than it had in previous years.

My husband lived with my parents for 6 months, helping them to rebuild their home. My daughter was still in high school but was going to a charter school only a few days a week which allowed us to travel back and forth to help and see my husband.

I believe that God works in mysterious ways because my husband's company was in the construction industry and business was slow, allowing him the time to go help my parents maneuver through the insurance adjusters. The whole bit to get the home rebuilt.

While spending more time with my parents, my bond with

my dad became stronger. As his health weakened, I would lay next to him while he rested in his bed, and we would discuss scripture.

He wasn't a perfect man for sure, as none of us are, and yet there was no doubt he loved Jesus. It was always evident what was most important to him, and I value this example in my memories of growing up.

Those last 6 months of his life we often talked about Philippians 4:8 and what we should be focused on- the pure, the true, and the right – and to think about those things.

I knew his time was ending soon, when a couple of weeks prior to his death, while getting close to finishing up their home, I took Dad in his wheelchair to show him the design ideas I had for the backyard landscaping. He was not the least bit interested. He said to me, "Honey, I don't care what you do, it's not important to me anymore".

Seeing him prepared to leave earth was comforting, although difficult for the rest of us. We all knew how much he would be missed.

I overheard mom tell him several times that she wasn't ready to let him go, that he "couldn't go yet". Mom has a strong belief in the afterlife, in heaven, but it is never easy to say goodbye to your loved ones.

I knew that people who are dying are helped when they know we who are left behind can let them go and release them. It is hard to be selfless and let someone go, yet Dad had told me many times he was ready. He was ready for no more pain and no more sorrow.

One Sunday a couple of weeks before Dad's passing, I was with him in the hospital, while my mom was at church with my sister. Dad was laying in bed and I know he was talking to Jesus.

I could overhear him saying as he moaned in pain, "Please take me". I thought that day would be his last.

The doctors came in and told me everything they could do to try to keep Dad alive. I knew he didn't want that. I told them so. It didn't seem like they understood and yet I remember standing firm to support my dad's wishes and letting the doctor and the nurses know that he didn't want any more tests or medicines. That was when they talked about home health care or hospice.

Mom returned to the hospital and I gave them space to be alone. She had just come from church and I know she was feeling stronger. I watched them embrace each other, and then I heard Mom whisper, "It's ok to go, I love you."

Dad died August 6, 2013, on their 53rd anniversary.

After Dad died, I was a mess. I had experienced death before. My brother died in 1993 at 31 years old, but this was different. This was my dad.

Most people didn't know I was a mess because I kept it hidden. I am sure some of you can relate to that. We get good at putting on a happy face, going through the motions of life, and making social media look like life's all great. We only post the good in our lives, or the "highlight reels." We hide what is really happening.

It appeared that I had it all under control, that I was strong, that I totally could handle all that was happening on my own. And yet I wasn't.

How often has someone asked you how you are, and you instantly respond with a smile and say, "I'm fine", or "I'm good?"

That doesn't work so well, does it? Bottled-up emotions don't just disappear; they build up, leading to chronic stress, sadness, or numbness.

Grief is hard. Losing a loved one can be one of the most difficult experiences in a person's life. Coping with grief can seem like a difficult task at times, and overcoming grief can seem impossible.

I don't believe we ever overcome per se, we just learn to live differently.

I knew that instead of learning how to overcome grief I needed to learn how to embrace the emotions I was experiencing.

I was sad. I was mad at times. I felt lonely knowing I would never get a burly, bear hug from my dad ever again. Yet I also knew Dad would want me to live life, in a new way, without him, yet having learned from him.

He would want me to move ahead and know joy and peace in this life.

Moving ahead, to me, acknowledges that life continues, but it doesn't dismiss the grief or the love that remains when we lose someone in our lives.

Moving ahead implies progress, growth, and finding a way to live with the loss while still honoring the person.

It is important not to pressure someone to get over their grief, but instead encourage them to keep going, carrying their memories and love forward in a way that feels right for them.

It's a gentle reminder that healing isn't about forgetting, it's about learning to live in a new way while keeping our loved ones in our hearts.

So, I did. I began looking for joy in my days. I knew that was the choice I wanted to make.

Instead of trying to overcome grief, what if we learned how to have this season of life, become a part of our story?

What if I just started writing about all that I was feeling? And

PREFACE

maybe, just maybe, my story could help someone else. Maybe my story would encourage other people to seek God in their own journey, and they too could have more peace and joy in their lives even during hard times.

It is possible.

CHAPTER 1
I HAD IT ALL PLANNED...

"Many are the plans in a person's heart, but it is the LORD's purpose that prevails." (Prov. 19:21 NIV)

One of the first things I did after dad's passing was really evaluate my life.

I had been working for years as a financial advisor. It had taken me a while to gain all the federal and state licensing to become an advisor, sometimes having to take the tests multiple times before finally getting a "PASS". So much effort, and even tears had gone into that accomplishment.

I so remember missing one of the exams by one stinking point, and I went to my car and just cried and cried. I was so discouraged. But I kept at it and eventually passed.

We all go through things that are really hard. For some it is losing a loved one, for others it could be a health diagnosis, or a troubled marriage that leads to divorce. Maybe for you it's dealing with past trauma that keeps showing up and affecting your life in ways you never imagined.

Or you go to college and spend years getting a degree only to realize you can't find a job. Or you start a business, and it flops.

Life can be hard and yet somehow, we keep going.

Like being an advisor. It took me so much effort and time and yet I wasn't happy in that industry.

Thankfully, my husband wins the award for being so supportive. He encouraged me after dad died to really think about what I wanted to do. What direction did God want me to go?

How often do we think we know the direction our life is supposed to go, only to realize we are headed a whole different way?

This makes me think of a time my husband and I were headed to the San Francisco International airport.

My husband put the address into the app.

He couldn't quite figure out why it had him go on streets we never traveled, just to get to the freeway. I suggested he just follow it. He's impatient. He's sure his way is better.

Why? Because it's familiar. It's what he's used to.

And yet I encouraged him to just trust the app.

And sure enough, it took us on these roads to reduce time, traffic, and too many lights. I reminded him we were also seeing places in our own town we had never seen in 30 years.

And I thought about life.

We often wonder why our "road" isn't working, why it hasn't been the fastest route, why we have had to have so many detours? And yet, what if we were willing to trust the "app"? Or trust advice or encouragement from others. Or better yet, have patience and know that God is in control, that He will lead us, in His timing, to where we are to go.

Don't get stuck in life because you're not willing to open your mind to new perspectives, new opportunities.

Maybe up ahead is something so much greater. Life will always bring changes, and often, those changes end up being just what we need.

For me, that change was becoming a Certified Life and Health Coach.

Which then led to me writing this book.

If you have been struggling through life, wishing things were different, and yet just not sure what to do, I want you to hear this: *YOU can change your life, by changing the way you respond to life.*

HERE ARE three journal prompts to help you reflect on the theme of this chapter:

1. **Plans vs. Purpose:** Think about a time when you had everything planned out, only for life to take a different turn. What did that detour teach you about trusting a higher purpose? How does Proverbs 19:21 speak to that experience in your life?
2. **Embracing Detours:** Reflect on a moment when things didn't go as expected, like when you took an unexpected route and discovered something new. What did that change reveal to you about your path or about trusting the journey, even when it's not what you had planned?
3. **Changing Your Response:** Consider a challenging period when you felt stuck or overwhelmed. How did changing the way you responded to that challenge help you move forward? What new perspective did you gain about life and your future when you let go of rigid plans?

These prompts are designed to encourage you to see that even when things don't go as planned, there is a purpose at work, guiding you toward a richer, more fulfilling journey. Enjoy the reflection!

CHAPTER 2
WHAT GRIEF TEACHES US: LESSONS IN LOVE AND LOSS

My flesh and my heart may fail, but God is the strength of my heart and my portion forever. (Ps. 73:26 NIV)

Most likely, we will experience grief more than once in our lifetime.

Grief is not always just a response to death, such as me losing my dad and my brother.

It's a response to loss. It could be losing a loved one; it could be losing friendships, relationships, identities. For some it could be the loss of a pet, or a job, or even the feeling of losing stability.

Another grief I experienced recently was leaving the church that my husband and I had attended my entire life.

I have wonderful memories in that church. I loved our annual church "conventions", our weekly Bible studies, the connection, and the community. I loved the memories of my parents hosting a Sunday meeting once a month in our home and families coming over for lunch and dessert. I have wonderful friends all over the world who I met because of that time of my life. I loved memories of traveling to other states and having fellowship with others. It was special.

One day, we heard of an immense amount of abuse that had happened in the church. How could this be? We began hearing about child sexual abuse and sexual abuse in churches in alarming amounts all over the world.

People we knew, people we trusted, were not who we thought they were. Some were the abusers and others had covered it up and kept it secret for years.

I, fortunately, was not a victim of sexual abuse, but I was groomed.

When I was 16, I was dating a guy from the church, and we were helping his family move. There was a minister helping us and I knew this guy was acting very inappropriately around me when we were taking boxes and their belongings into one of the bedrooms.

Thankfully, after that weekend of moving, I told my mom. And she believed me. Thank God.

I will never forget that she did what we thought was the right thing and she "reported" it, not to authorities, but rather to one of the head ministers of the church. That was what we knew to do at the time, expecting that this behavior wouldn't continue with other young girls. Sadly, it did.

For years after that, I would see this guy, who was still in the ministry for many more years, at our church conventions and I would avoid him.

Eventually, he was out of the work ministry. And he got married. I would see him with his wife and children at the church conventions, and I would pray for his children, hoping they were safe.

My husband and I both felt in the deepest parts of our hearts that we had a responsibility to do whatever we could to help anyone who had been a victim - to listen, care for, support and believe their stories.

Many of our friends and family did not understand why we were leaving the church, and I had to be okay with that. We had to listen to God and be moved by what we felt God was asking us to do.

I will never forget my Hobby Lobby moment when I was sitting in my car in the parking lot praying. For some reason during this season, I would pray a lot in my car. I was alone and it felt right.

I was praying, and begging God to help me, to help us, know what direction we were supposed to go.

And wow, talk about the fastest answered prayer.

Almost immediately as I sat there. I felt like God was talking right to me and saying, "Darla, you will only answer to me, not to anyone else, just me, so I need you to listen and go be obedient"

I am so thankful for that moment, that clarification.

I am grateful for all the support we have seen, so many willing to step up and do what they can. It's truly incredible the amount of people being open to helping others; a true testament of love and grace towards others.

It became so real to me in the midst of this hard experience, that we all have different "gifts" and "talents". If I wasn't using my gift that I feel God gave to me to encourage others, it would be as though I had buried it.

And I knew from scripture that this was something I was not willing to do.

I was not going to bury it. In Matthew 25, the parable of the buried talents refers to a story where a servant, given a talent (a unit of money) by his master, chooses to bury it in the ground instead of using it to generate more wealth. This represents the idea of not utilizing one's God-given abilities or gifts to their full potential; essentially, being lazy and not actively using what you have been given.

What kept standing out to me about this scripture as I was reading it during this difficult season was that the man in this scripture even refers to being afraid, so that's why he buried it.

How often in our lives has something come up and it causes us to be afraid? We don't know what to do, so we do nothing. We bury it. And because we bury it, it gets worse.

So often when people bury things, it can influence their entire lives. Even their health.

I am no one special. I had no idea what I was supposed to be doing. And yet, I knew to pray. I begged God for guidance and help.

The amount of grief that so many have experienced has been heart wrenching. We all had put so much trust in man, in a church. We needed to learn that our hope and confidence had to be in Jesus, and in Jesus alone.

I found so much comfort in the beginning of that season, when God clearly told me to "Go do whatever brings you closer to me". I had no idea what that even looked like or will continue to look like for my future.

One of the things I started doing is attending CBS, a Community Bible Study, an international bible study where we study only scripture. There is no church affiliation, and I could meet a community of women who love learning about Jesus and the Word of God. I love this because it's not about what church someone attends, or doesn't, it's not about a pastor, it's only about the Word of God.

I have learned that there is/was so much I do not know about Jesus. And my greatest desire is to know him better.

I love knowing that our journeys are so personal; it's our story, no one else's. We each will stand before God, alone. I love knowing that God will lead us closer to Him during these difficult experiences if we have an honest heart and really seek His purpose in our lives.

Grief will be different for each of us. How we respond or react will be different. I am not saying the way I responded was the best way, nor the only way; and yet it was what God was leading me to do.

I WANT to share what has helped me deal with different types of grief:

1. **Remember and celebrate the life of your loved one.** An important part of healing is allowing yourself to talk about the memories you have of your loved one.
2. **Acknowledge Your Feelings.** Grief is often a very hard experience. Everyone responds differently. It is wise to remember that even everyone in your family might not respond or react the way you do. That is ok. There really is no right way. Grief can be such a painful experience that sometimes people purposely avoid their feelings rather than address how they are feeling on the inside. When it comes to grief, avoidance does not work. Avoiding grief may seem like the best thing to do at the time, but the pain awaits you, and eventually, it needs to be faced and experienced.
3. **Take care of yourself.** Taking care of oneself looks very different for each of us. One person might benefit by having time alone, whereas someone else needs to be surrounded by loved ones. Maybe for you, it's having a massage, or just going to lunch with a girlfriend. I fell somewhere in the middle. I loved being with people

and yet I truly loved time alone, too. I feel it is key to respect the feelings of others in this situation.

4. **Stick to healthy habits.** An important part will be in making sure you take care of yourself. This includes eating healthy and getting exercise. Sometimes depression, anxiety, and physical symptoms of grief will result in an unhealthy diet and even a lack of desire to eat. Avoid too much sugar, empty carbs, as well as drinking alcohol, or at least overdrinking. If you are only able to eat in small amounts during the first days of grief, that's ok. Show kindness to yourself and choose to eat foods that will bring you energy and make you feel better versus consuming foods that will only hinder your ability to heal properly. Exercise is an important part of the healing process. It will give you a natural boost. When it is incorporated into our daily routine, we will see how it positively benefits depression and the grief experience. Exercise will not cure grief, but it is a healthy method of dealing with difficult emotions when they arise. One thing that has helped me in all the varying periods of grief has been walking. There is so much healing in being outside in nature, getting my steps in for the day. I often pray while walking, of course, with my eyes open! When I was dealing with dad's passing away, I would walk for miles, listening to Christian radio, and just enjoying nature all around.

5. **Give yourself grace because grief is unpredictable.** Feelings and emotions around grief will come out of nowhere, and often when you don't expect it. There is not a magical number of days, months, or even years when you will "get over" grief. No one should expect

that of you. A few weeks after my father passed away, we were busy working on rebuilding a home for my mom. One day I was at Home Depot, and for some reason, emotions took over and I was sobbing in the plumbing department. I literally sat on a toilet display and cried…I am sure I was quite the sight to those walking by. Allow yourself grace when you find yourself suddenly crying, even when you least expect it. It's ok. And even in the beginning stages of the church grief, I cried a lot. What I love remembering though are the times when I was so desperate for help, that I found myself on the ground, praying and begging God for answers, for direction, for help, and how much peace would come over me.

6. **Be patient with yourself and others.** Grieving takes time. There is no shortcut around it. It is a natural process we experience when we care deeply for someone who has died. Maybe for you, the grief isn't the loss of someone, but rather the loss of a job, pet, or community. Offer yourself the love, kindness, compassion and patience that you would give to a friend. Remember this for other family and friends who may have lost someone as well or are going through grief in other areas of their lives. As I mentioned previously, we all respond differently to grief and life experiences, so being patient with people who make different choices than we do is key. It's their life, their decision.

7. **Reach out to others who may be experiencing grief as well.** Everyone will experience grief in their lives at some point. I have found that by being open to sharing with others, we can often find encouragement and it

can bring about hope and healing. I was talking to someone recently whose father had passed away. He didn't talk about it much. One day his mom mentioned she wished someone would talk about her husband, his dad. He realized that day that there could be healing in being vulnerable, not just for himself, but also for his mom. Maybe grief for you is in a relationship or a friendship that has changed. What has helped me is to have the conversation, or at least try, and recognize that some friendships in life are for a season, or a chapter in our life, and then things change. I have had to do this even recently with people that I love and have been a part of my entire life, but our friendships have changed. I have had to come to an understanding that for now, at least, it's going to be different. What has been so amazing to me, is that although my choices led to a few friendships changing, God has brought me a lot of new people I enjoy being with. For that I'm grateful.

8. **Seek out support.** Seeking support is crucial during times of grief. Support can come from friends, family, grief support groups, grief counselors, and online support options. I personally have enjoyed volunteering at our local Jessica's House, a Grief Recovery Center, where they create a safe place for children, teens, young adults, and their families who are grieving a death, providing hope and healing to our community.

9. **Accept the new place you are in.** This can take time and yet you will often find that by realizing the place you are now in, you can help others, you can even begin to see the blessings in the experience, and the

learning. I never would have imagined that my experiences of losing my brother when I was a young mom and then later my father, would lead to me helping others on their grief journey. I am thankful for that.

HEALING

When I think back on the grief I experienced after losing my dad, I had a dream that began the mental, physical, and spiritual healing I desperately needed.

I love that God has spoken to me many times in my lifetime through dreams. I don't always understand them, yet often there is great learning in them.

This dream, nine months after my dad died, changed my life.

My husband and I were away for a few days and sleeping in a trailer. As I was sleeping, I was dreaming about my father. He was telling me that it was time to move on, to let him go, and to promise him that I would. To go be happy, to live life, and to share more about Jesus with others. And so, out loud, I said, "I will". My husband heard me and I awoke to a wet pillow because I had been crying in my dream.

I let Dad "go" that day…now it's not that I didn't miss him ever again, and yet the heaviness of heart, the gloomy feelings I had had, for nine months, subsided. Instead of being sad, I began THINKING about the pure, the right, the just. I began focusing my thoughts on what I knew to be true instead of living in sadness.

This was exactly what my dad would've hoped for me.

This topic of our thoughts became something I really wanted to learn more about for myself, to study, and to share with others. I knew there had to be something really powerful to learn about how our thoughts influence every single area of our lives.

One of my greatest and most cherished memories of the last six months of my dad's life was him quoting this verse to me:

Philippians 4:8 NIV

"Finally, brothers and sisters, whatever is true, whatever is noble, whatever is right, whatever is pure, whatever is lovely, whatever is admirable—if anything is excellent or praiseworthy—think about such things."

This verse is what became my focus for my own life and heart, and it became the catalyst for my life coaching practice. I knew that if I could change my own life through changing how I think that others could too. I wanted to be available to help others on their own journey.

To help them to think about what is right, pure, honest…

HERE ARE three journal prompts to help you dive deeper into the lessons of grief:

1. **Rediscovering Strength Through Loss:** Reflect on a time when grief—whether from the loss of a person, a relationship, or even a familiar place—changed the way you saw life. How did that experience help you lean on God's strength, as reminded in Psalm 73:26 (NIV) "My flesh and my heart may fail, but God is the strength of my heart and my portion forever"? What did you learn about your inner resilience during that time?
2. **Transforming Pain into Purpose:** Think about the ways grief has reshaped your understanding of love and loss. How did a difficult chapter in your life lead

you to discover new gifts or a deeper sense of purpose? Write about a moment when you realized that even in the midst of pain, there was a chance to grow and help others with your experience.

3. **Shifting Your Focus to What Truly Matters:** Philippians 4:8 encourages us to dwell on whatever is true, noble, right, pure, lovely, and admirable. In moments of deep sorrow, how have you managed—or how could you begin—to redirect your thoughts toward these qualities? What practical steps might you take to nurture this positive focus in your daily life, even when grief feels overwhelming?

These prompts are meant to guide you in exploring the personal lessons and growth that grief can bring. Enjoy the reflection, and know that every chapter of your life, even the painful ones, have something valuable to teach you.

CHAPTER 3
LISTENING TO MY BODY: WHEN HEALTH AND MINDSET COLLIDE

"In their hearts humans plan their course, but the Lord establishes their steps." Prov. 16:9, NIV

We were living in our dream house that we had built by ourselves in 2006. Our boys were teens when we built the house, and it was an awesome learning experience. My husband was able to teach them how to dig trenches, frame the walls, and help with so much of the building. It was a lot of hard work, and sweat, yet we loved it.

We loved that house. We loved having company all the time, and pool parties. We even hosted a two-day weekend of fun for our teens and about 50 other kids where they did a neighborhood scavenger hunt. It was a hoot. I remember that all the things the kids found, they had to not only mark off, but bring them back to the house. One item on the list was a bald man with brown shoes! Yes, they brought him too.

I love the memories there. At least most of them. Life seemed to be going along just as we had planned it to be, or so we thought. But life doesn't always happen how we want it to, right? We thought we had it all figured out.

When we were building that house, it was valued at $1.3 million. The market was booming and often people would stop by and want to know if we would sell it to them.

Ha, no, it's going to be our house. We were so excited as our kids were the perfect age - the boys were in their teens, and our daughter was six years younger than her brothers. It truly was a great time of life.

(Looking back, hello, yes, we should have sold it…but hindsight is crystal clear, right?)

Now it's 2009-10, and the economy was crashing all around. It was common to drive down the road and see many homes with dead lawns because the families who owned them had lost their jobs and therefore couldn't pay their mortgages and would just walk away from a mortgage they couldn't afford.

Our home was worth $1.3 million when we built it. And now not even four years later, it was worth $500,000.

We were knee-deep in debt, we were buying groceries on credit and using our second mortgage to help with the bills. The crazy part was we had one of those crazy mortgages that gave you payment options and because of the financial straits we were in, we often paid the payment that was less than interest. (Not something I would suggest at all!)

I was living a life of complete stress wondering how in the world we were going to get out from under our current reality. My dear husband had lost a lot of income during that period and yet, thankfully, had not been laid off.

I was still working as a financial advisor then. Talk about stress. Not only were we personally having financial challenges, but many of my clients' 401k's were in the tank.

Maybe some of you reading this remember that time. Maybe

you foreclosed on your home or lost your job and wondered how to pay the bills or feed the family.

I was living with continuous headaches, my body was aching, I was tired all the time. Yet I kept up the appearance of having it all together.

Do you see a common thread here? Remember back to when my dad died and I put on this false front that all was well? Friends, hiding our emotions, burying them, only leads to health issues.

I will never forget standing in the shower, my beautiful, big shower of our lovely master bedroom, the water just pouring down my head and realizing that the left side of my body was numb.

I went to the doctor and had a bunch of tests done. Thankfully the tests showed normal.

And yet, I was still feeling lousy. I don't know if you have ever experienced that. It's frustrating, yet you are grateful, too, that they can't find anything.

I later was referred to a Rheumatologist who did some more testing and did tell me they thought based on some blood work and how much my body was hurting, that I had Rheumatoid Arthritis.

This honestly wasn't too surprising to me. My paternal grandma died at 68 years old from complications of Rheumatoid Arthritis. I can totally see my grandma in my mind, even at the young age I was. (I think I was about 10 when she died.) Her fingers were totally crippled, and she lived on a bunch of medications. They lived in the Midwest so many winters they would escape the cold and come visit us in California. She always arrived with a suitcase that is typically meant for toiletries, except hers was loaded with medications. She always seemed old to me and as I aged, I realized how young 68 was to have passed away.

I knew that I did not want to die that young, and I was determined, if possible, to not live on medications. I had kids to raise, I wanted to see them graduate, get married, have their own families. I wanted to be a grandma.

The doctor proceeded to give me a prescription that day for medication that would potentially slow down the process of RA. I immediately gave it right back to her.

(Now, a little disclaimer here, I am not a doctor, and of course, I know that there is a time and place for medications, and yet, for me, on that day, at that time of my life, I made a decision to do something else first.)

I left the doctor's office that day and never returned to that one. I left with a renewed purpose to make changes for my health. I had no idea what that meant, but I knew I had to make changes.

Remember, we were broke. I was stressed from all the challenges we were experiencing, so I couldn't just run out and join a gym. I knew that one thing I needed to do for my stress was get outside and exercise. So, I walked, and I walked.

I remember people telling me they would see me passing by as my ponytail swished from side to side. I think it's important to mention that most people had no idea we were experiencing all this…I was too prideful to admit our situation.

One of the first things I did, I have no idea why, is I started reading a book originally published in the early 1950's, called The Power of Positive Thinking, by Norman Vincent Peale. I love this book, and I refer it to most of my clients. It's spiritually based and refers to scripture often.

This is a sentence that woke me up.

"How we THINK we feel, has a definite effect on how we actually feel physically."

Wow, this totally goes with that scripture I shared at the beginning of the book from Phillipians 4:8 NIV.

Finally, brothers and sisters, whatever is true, whatever is noble, whatever is right, whatever is pure, whatever is lovely, whatever is admirable—if anything is excellent or praiseworthy—think about such things.

There it was. I needed to "flip the switch" of how I was thinking.

It was a choice I could make.

Say what? So potentially, my health, how I was feeling with the headaches, body aches, all the things, could be made worse by the stress and anxiety I was feeling and the way I was thinking?

I had never thought much about how our thoughts, how we think and even how we talk to ourselves, and others can affect our lives, our health, our relationships.

So, you mean that when I was constantly, even if it's just in my head, telling myself things such as "We will never get out of this mess" or "Life sucks" that this was only making it worse? Making me worse?

People don't often stop to realize how much their thoughts, their worry is totally influencing their lives. I totally had not thought about this, and I was ready to change.

I wanted to feel better. I wanted to know peace.

Worrying is a normal part of the human experience that I am pretty sure we all have experienced in our lives. Have you ever known someone who was referred to as a "Worry Wart"?

If we leave it unchecked, it can begin to have detrimental effects on our physical health and our mental health.

What exactly is worrying? Well according to my Google search on the definition it says this: *Noun, a state of anxiety and uncertainty over actual or potential problems. Verb, give way to anxiety or unease; allow one's mind to dwell on difficulty or troubles.*

Maybe you're worried over a presentation you have to give tomorrow, or you worry you might have a serious health condition in the future. Or maybe you wonder how to put food on the table for your family.

It's not easy to rid yourself of these thoughts completely, yet it is possible to reduce their negative effects significantly.

A FEW THINGS I do for myself that help me reduce my worry:

1. **Breathing.** I have a few ways that I do this mindfully. One way that I find really helps is to do this: Sit in a chair, with both feet on the floor. You can close your eyes if you need to. Breathe IN what you want (i.e. love, peace, joy, understanding, kindness, etc.) and breathe OUT what you don't want (frustration, worry, anger, tiredness, whatever words come up for you) and do this 3 times.
2. **Talk it Out.** Is there someone who you can confide your concerns to? My husband is always able to help me see different perspectives. Or is there someone who doesn't give any advice but just listens and shows they care.
3. **Turn Your Thoughts Around.** Ask yourself if what you are worried about has ever happened before. What are the chances of it truly happening? And take the necessary action to change the way you think about it.

One of the best things I have ever done was to begin giving my thoughts to God. Realizing that God cares about every single part of our life. He cares about my emotions, my tears, my angst, and He can help us learn to let go and know more peace in the midst of the storm.

I seem to do my "best" worrying in bed in the middle of the night. It's almost like God is reminding me, "Hello, I am right here, just waiting for you to give me that concern".

One of the areas of the Power of the Positive Thinking is where the author describes on page 114-115, what he refers to as the process of "mind drainage".

He mentions not being discouraged, for you can overcome your worries and how doing this process you can break the worry habit. The first step he mentions is believing that you can. And how with God's help, you can do anything.

He encourages us to practice emptying our mind daily, preferably before we head to bed, in the last five minutes before going to sleep.

Here is what he says in his book, "This process of mind drainage is important in overcoming worry, for fear thoughts, unless drained off, can clog the mind, impede the flow of mental and spiritual power. But such thoughts can be emptied from the mind and will not accumulate if they are eliminated daily. To drain them, utilize a process of creative imagination. Conceive of yourself as actually emptying your mind of all anxiety and fear. Picture all worry thoughts as flowing out as you would let a water flow from a basin by removing the stopper. Repeat the following affirmation during this visualization. "" With God's help, I am now emptying my mind of all anxiety, all fear, all sense of insecurity."" Repeat this slowly five times, then add, "" I believe that my mind is now emptied of all anxiety, all fear, all sense of insecurity."" Repeat that statement 5 times, meanwhile holding a mental picture of your mind as being emptied of these concepts. Then thank God for thus freeing you from fear. Then go to sleep."

I have done this myself many times over the years, as well as sharing this idea with my clients. They too, have felt calm come over them as they commit their anxiety and worry to God and it allows them to sleep more peacefully.

You will find, as I have, that some days you will be really good at it, and other days, well, not so much. It's ok. Don't give up.

Just the other day I was thinking about a verse that says, 1 Peter 5:7 New Living Translation, "Give all your worries and cares to God, for he cares about you." And then I read the verse prior in 1 Peter 5:6 (translation), "HUMBLE yourselves, therefore, under God's mighty hand, that he may lift you up in due time".

That really hit me - humble yourself. I was feeling pretty good about myself, ha, oh yeah, I give my cares to God...but humbly? Oops! Well, not all the time.

And I realized that is the key for me. To recognize I need help, I don't know it all, I don't know the future, but I know the one who does.

Years ago, when I was diagnosed with RA, I remember leaving the doctor's office realizing I had changes to make. I researched how some with RA are able to get help or at least lessen their pain. Not only was exercise and movement key, I also needed to drink more water, and pay attention to what I was eating. I knew that too much sugar and processed foods were not good for me. But I had no idea how much caffeine can affect autoimmune diseases. What I also didn't know at that time was how much worry, stress and anxiety affected health. I needed to be responsible for my health. I needed to stop making excuses.

Seriously, I want you to think about this for a moment. I bet you **KNOW** what you need to do, even for your own health, and yet so often we don't do it. Right?

Like I know I should take that walk or eat healthy food versus driving through the McDonald's drive thru again. Or how about this one...sitting down to watch a show while aimlessly eating an entire bag of your favorite crunch snack.

That last one is totally something I had been guilty of before. Those darn barbeque chips or crackers...I love crackers. I would say I am more of a carb lover than sweets.

We often make excuses for our lives. Well, if I wasn't in this situation, if I had a different job, if I had more time, if I made more money, then...

And yet those excuses, the time we are delaying, or honestly, wasting, could be used instead to get healthier. And I am not just talking about what we eat and drink.

I truly believe that we can be super strict on our exercise, and our eating, and yet if we don't deal with the inner man, what's really going on, if we don't let go of negative emotions, any trauma we might have, then we can lose weight, appear healthier, and yet still be miserable inside.

I knew for things to be different; I had to change. And I had to look differently at what that even meant.

What has been truly key to my health, to my transformation, to having energy, is how I THINK.

That might surprise you and yet I have proven this to myself.

I guarantee that if you consider your thoughts towards your health, if you consider what you are telling yourself on a daily basis, and begin telling yourself that you do have value, that you deserve to be healthy, know wellness, lose weight, or whatever wellness looks like for you, that is when you will start to see the changes you have been hoping for.

If you truly want to change your life, you first must be willing to change your <u>MIND!</u>

In *The Power of Positive Thinking* by Norman Vincent Peale, he writes, "A physician once said, 'Many of my patients have nothing wrong with them except their thoughts!'"

He goes on to say, "So I have a favorite prescription that I write for some, but it is not a prescription that you can fill at a drugstore. The prescription I write is a verse from the Bible—Romans 12:2. I do not write out that verse for my patients; I make them look it up, and it reads: 'Be ye transformed by the renewing of your mind.'

"To be happier and healthier, they need a renewing of their minds—that is, a change in the pattern of their thoughts. When they 'take' this prescription, they actually achieve a mind full of peace. That helps to produce health and well-being."

Seriously, I didn't like reading that. But for me, I knew it was true.

But it made sense, because often in my lifetime when I had been experiencing headaches, tiredness, anxiety, there wasn't anything "medically" wrong with me.

I felt like I was a fairly positive person and yet I also knew I had been disconnecting from my feelings. I was often avoiding what was really going on and how I was really feeling, but all this was doing was leading to toxicity.

I actually had a lady tell me one time that I was too positive and I was avoiding how I really was.

I honestly was a bit irritated with her for saying that, and yet I knew it was true. It's more than being "positive", putting on a front of positivity. For me, I knew I needed to work on my inner man.

I knew from all my research, book reading, and even verses I found in scripture, that our minds are powerful.

We are all living in our CPR, our CURRENT PERCEIVED REALITY. You have what you have, you know what you know, you do what you do…

What you want, the new results, more energy, a smaller number on the scale, this is your NDR (NEW DESIRED RESULT)

What is in between is your BELIEF GAP.

Until you bridge the gap, you will stay where you are. We need to learn to have expectations and believe in what you want.

We make our decisions based on the information we have. In order to make new decisions, we need new information.

Read that again.

We make our decisions based on the information we have. If you want different results, different outcomes, my friend, you need new information.

I have thought of that saying so much in the last two years. Often, we will make decisions, and they aren't necessarily wrong, but are they the best for us?

Have you ever considered how many decisions you have made because that is what your lifelong reality has been? That is what your family has always done?

And we begin to realize that by being open to new information, whether we gain it from prayer, book knowledge, scripture, or life experiences, we then see that maybe it is time for new decisions.

So often when people hire me to coach them, they might come initially to lose weight, wear a certain size, have better relationships, learn how to enjoy life. Soon they are aware that in order to do those things, in order to lose weight and actually keep it off, or to even have better marriages, they have to begin to look at life differently. They need to be open to opportunities and ideas that will help them to get results that maybe they never experienced before.

What is amazing is that it often begins with something as simple as beginning to have *gratitude* in even loving themselves exactly where they are today.

Being willing to accept that maybe you made some wrong decisions in the past, and that is ok. What matters now is where you are going from here.

Accept that where you are right now is where you are. Love it, be grateful for it, and be willing to move on with new information.

Learn to bridge that gap.

Do you love yourself? (This isn't a love, like "I am so great". This is a love for the person God created - you - the unique YOU.) Do you have gratitude for yourself? Do you have childhood insecurities that are holding you back from having the results you want in your life? Are you holding on to something your parents said to you? Maybe it was a teacher, relative, or a bully at school.

Maybe you were told you were fat as a child? I have had clients who were told really cruel remarks as children, whether from kids at school or even family, and have struggled with weight their entire lives. Then one day they begin having success, yet they couldn't let go of the negative words. So, they held on to them and actually found comfort in staying a heavier weight.

I will never forget this coaching session from many years ago. A lady was telling me she was 80 pounds overweight. She had tried so many diets over the years. She would lose some, gain some, feel better about herself, and then get frustrated again. Sound familiar?

As we dove deeper in the session, she opened up that many years ago she had been in the Army and while there she had been attacked. She was young then, in shape, felt pretty, and then this happened. And her life changed drastically.

Here we were over 20 years later, and she needs to lose 80

pounds. And what became evident was that she was actually holding on to this weight because it made her feel safe. If she kept herself overweight, then bad things wouldn't happen to her. She had to work to release this trauma, to release the negative around the experience. It wasn't that this experience would just go away. Yet she would eventually get to where this horrible experience wouldn't control her life anymore. I loved watching her let go of the strong hold that this horrible experience had had on her.

We so often hold on to horrible experiences in our lives and they keep us stuck.

WHY DO WE DO THIS? Let's explore this more...

Emotional Impact: Traumatic or negative experiences often bring on strong emotions, and our brains are wired to remember emotionally charged events more vividly. This emotional intensity can make it challenging to let go.

Fear of Repetition: The fear of encountering similar negative experiences in the future may lead people to hold on to past traumas as a way of protecting themselves. This fear can create a mental loop that reinforces the negative memories. (As my client above was doing)

Sense of Identity: Some people derive a sense of identity or purpose from their struggles or traumas. Letting go of these experiences may feel like letting go of a part of oneself, which can be emotionally challenging.

Unresolved Issues: If the emotional wounds from a negative experience haven't been properly addressed or resolved, individuals may find it difficult to move on. Unresolved issues can linger in the subconscious and influence thoughts and behaviors.

Lack of Coping Mechanisms: If someone hasn't developed

healthy coping mechanisms or skills to process and overcome negative experiences, they may resort to holding on to these experiences as a way of dealing with them, even if it keeps them stuck.

Attachment to Victimhood: In some cases, individuals may develop an attachment to the role of the victim. This can provide a sense of justification for their emotions and actions, making it challenging to let go of the victim mentality.

Breaking free from the grip of terrible experiences is possible. It often requires the help of a medical professional, a coach, a therapist, support of loved ones as well as personal growth activities.

Just remember, it takes time, effort, and even grace towards yourself. And a desire to know change. Growth. Joy.

A desire to learn new information that will help you to make changes that will make you know more peace and joy in your heart.

I know you can do it...I have seen and helped hundreds of women do this.

So, I bet you're asking, "Well, how do I even begin having gratitude for myself when life seems to suck a lot of the time?"

Why is having a spirit of gratitude key to our lives?

The benefits of practicing gratitude are nearly endless. People who regularly practice gratitude by taking time to notice and reflect upon the things they're thankful for experience more positive emotions, feel more alive, sleep better, express more compassion and kindness, and even have stronger immune systems.

Studies have shown that gratitude has a direct effect on depression symptoms. People who practice daily gratitude in these studies shared that they felt less depressed. There was also an indirect effect on anxiety because when they increased their gratitude, they slept better which led to lower anxiety.

I know for myself, I have awoken in the middle of the night with feelings of anxiety, and I had to make a choice to focus on the anxiety or focus on gratitude.

It is not easy to do, trust me. It can be very difficult, actually.

I personally love scripture that speaks of having a spirit of gratitude.

Some that I have helped me are:

"Give thanks in all circumstances, for this is the will of God in Christ Jesus for you" (1 Thes. 5:18 English Standard Version)

"This is the day that the Lord has made; let us rejoice and be glad in it" (Ps. 118:24 ESV)

"And let the peace of Christ rule in your hearts, to which indeed you were called in one body. And be thankful." (Col. 3:15 ESV)

Now that you've read about the benefits of practicing gratitude, you may be wondering how you can start to add gratitude practice into your daily routine. I've chosen five of my favorite and fairly easy methods of practicing gratitude to share.

1. **Start a gratitude journal.** Find an old journal, or even use your phone, to start documenting what you are grateful for each day. It may be helpful to choose a specific time in the day to dedicate to your journaling. This can be as simple as writing down three things you are grateful for when you wake up, or picking one experience from the day to be thankful for before you go to bed. Don't overthink it! Start simple and you can always expand your practice as it becomes a habit. Your journal can just be a simple one from the dollar store or you can find great ones on Amazon. I personally love the 5 Minute Journal that I order online.

2. **Thank someone for something once a day.** Reach out to a

family member, friend, or coworker and thank them for something they've done, or just for being them! This can be as easy as sending a quick text or a five-minute phone call. Including someone else in your gratitude exercise is a great way to spread the effects of gratitude while also connecting in a unique way with someone in your life. You reap the benefits of practicing gratitude while making someone else's day- win win! I love doing this when I am having my quiet time in the morning, or even throughout the day, if I think of someone, I really make an effort to send a quick text or voice message to let them know. I truly believe that if someone comes to my heart, there is a reason. Think about how it makes you feel when someone reaches out to you because they thought of you, right?

3. **Make a gratitude jar**. Grab a recycled jar, box, or even a cup from your house and begin to write down one thing you are grateful for on a small slip of paper each day (or week if that feels easier) and throw it in the jar. This way you can slowly build a collection of gratitudes that you can go back and read when you're having a more challenging day. I have clients who do this with their kids and it's such a good example to teach this. We've done this before where I had a jar on my end table in the living room, with a pencil inside and a little note hanging from it. People other than our family even would see it and write down what they were grateful for. It was really neat to read over together at the end of the year. What was amazing was how many of the things we wrote down we had forgotten about and upon reading about them, it brought smiles to our faces and good memories.

4. **Write a kind review after a service**. Create a public thank you after you get a haircut or dine at a new restaurant. There are so many platforms to use today where we can leave reviews and recommendations on a product or service. Taking the time to do

this will allow you to really reflect on your recent experience, and reconnect with it, while also encouraging the company or individual behind the work. I always appreciate it when someone sends me testimonials after I have worked for them, so I like to reciprocate on this.

5. **Practice gratitude via mindfulness.** Sitting down and focusing on something you are grateful for or maybe focusing on how it feels in your body to be full of gratitude, and connecting to your breath is another great way to practice. The goal is to be present with the feeling or thought of gratitude to allow yourself to experience it to the fullest. One way I love doing this is when I am out walking, to purposely notice the flowers, the birds, the beauty around me. It helps get my thoughts on things other than maybe what I would be worried about, or the to-do list, the rush of life.

(As I sit writing this, I am outside, and birds are chirping, I am hearing the rustle of some trees in the wind, I am noticing a butterfly flying by me and the beauty of the Wisteria growing on the fence.)

Having gratitude won't always be easy. Just know that. I noticed a few months back as I went through the motions of doing my daily gratitude "habit" (more on habits in the second half of my book), writing my three things I am grateful for each day, I found I was really struggling with it. Some days it was a struggle to come up with even one.

Why was this? There were even a few days where I didn't even think to pick up my gratitude journal.

This was happening because my focus was on the current struggle, the experience I was in the midst of.

I know that what I focus on, expands. So, I allowed myself that space for a while, and then I got back at it. I know it makes me feel so much better when I begin my day thanking God for all

I have in my life. Even the hard stuff.

Is this something you have ever tried? Has it helped?

And so this morning, I was so thankful for a verse I came across at 3:30 am that says, Deuteronomy 31:8 New Living Translation 8 **Do not be afraid or discouraged**, for the Lord will personally go ahead of you. He will be with you; he will neither fail you nor abandon you."

Life will often bring some really hard stuff, right? Some you would never expect.

Makes me think of what I learned years ago in my NLP certification program (Nuerolinguistic Programming). It was not easy to swallow and yet I get it.

We are 100% responsible for our RESPONSE to life.

This might make you feel mad as you read this.

Does this mean that even when really terrible things happen that I am still responsible for my response to life?

That is not easy to hear. To digest.

This perspective suggests that while we may not have control over external events, we always have control over how we choose to react to them.

We may not be able to control what happens to us, but we have a choice in how we respond emotionally and mentally.

I have noticed since learning this and practicing myself, that it helps so I can respond to life versus react.

I like to think that reacting is emotional whereas responding is emotional intelligence.

If you are not familiar with what NLP is, it's a method of communication and personal development that aims to help individuals achieve their goals by changing their thought patterns and behaviors.

And it works.

So, inside our brains, we have neural pathways which are

formed over time. They are patterns of thinking that develop like train tracks which have a start point and the same destination. These thoughts follow pathways without even a conscious decision.

It's like my morning routine (Or as I will share later in the book, my HEALTHY HABITS). I don't even think about getting up, drinking my water, putting my contacts in, making my morning protein shake, and heading over to read my bible and do my gratitude journal.

This habit didn't happen overnight. It took weeks of consistency, and a desire for change.

But what I love is that we have the power and our brains have the neuroplasticity to redirect any negative trains of thoughts we might have.

Why is everyone else more successful than me?...

I will never learn from this…

Why can't I be like _____?...

…I can create new patterns of thinking.

God has given us the ability to do this.

I know without God's help, I would not be very successful at this.

When something goes wrong, I can recognize it as my learning or my limitation and seek God to help me gain more wisdom around this.

We can break free from these troubling thoughts that pop up from time to time.

This doesn't mean we will always be happy. And yet our emotional well-being is our capacity, our willingness, to allow ourselves to feel all our feelings. To admit, to yourself even, that we are struggling, to acknowledge our emotions, and then choose the best way to navigate through them.

This approach is not about denying the impact of life's

hardships or trauma; it's about understanding that, even in difficult situations, we have the ability to choose our attitude and actions.

I love knowing that how I am feeling emotionally, won't affect how God shows up for me, but it might affect how I show up for God

What has helped me is to slow down my thinking and identify them.

I have to ask myself some thought provoking questions like, "Does this type of thinking even align with the gifts that God has given me?"

Is this thinking taking me down a negative hole?

Is this way of thinking making me feel insecure, proud, defeated, less than?

Then I have to learn to CAPTURE those negative thoughts - I can't let them stay there as they truly do not belong.

In 2 Corinthians 10:5, it speaks of "taking every thought captive".

I am so grateful for that verse. And I have to remind myself to give that verse authority and declare it to myself. My mind needs to hear God's truth so my faith can increase.

So that the lies I am telling myself don't stay in my head.

And then I don't want to give up on this journey. It can take weeks, even months to renew patterns of thinking that have been stuck there for a while.

But if we are patient, we will see amazing changes in our minds. The important part is not to give up.

Earlier this week, I was having a session with a client, and she became aware that her ability to see life differently now, to "flip the switch" sooner while in the midst of difficult experiences or challenges, is becoming shorter. She's not staying stuck anymore.

She's doing the work. And boy does it show.

It personally took me years to really see how this was influencing my life too, and I really don't believe it's something we ever fully conquer.

And yet, with practice, you will begin to see that in life situations, you look for the good. You realize that even the really hard experiences, that we can, with the help of God, get through them.

HERE ARE **three journal prompts to help you dive into the themes of listening to your body and transforming your mindset:**

1. **Connecting Body and Mind:** Reflect on a time when you felt that your body was sending you a message—whether it was stress, pain, or fatigue. What were the circumstances? How did you respond at the time, and what might you do differently now knowing that your thoughts and mindset play a big role in your overall health?
2. **Challenging Negative Thought Patterns:** Think about some of the recurring worries or negative thoughts you've had—perhaps thoughts like "Why can't I be like others?" or "I'll never get out of this mess." How have these thoughts affected your health or energy levels? Write down one negative thought and then reframe it into a positive affirmation, inspired by the idea of "capturing every thought" (2 Corinthians 10:5). What steps can you take to make this new thought a part of your daily routine?
3. **Embracing New Information and Habits:** Consider a moment when you decided to change something in

your life—whether it was starting a gratitude journal, taking daily walks, or even changing how you ate. How did this new habit or information transform your mindset and physical well-being? What is one small, new habit you can adopt today to help bridge the gap between where you are now and the healthier, more peaceful life you desire?

These prompts are designed to help you reflect on the interplay between your physical health and your mindset, and to encourage you to be intentional about the thoughts and habits that shape your life. Enjoy the process!

CHAPTER 4
STRESS AND ITS SNEAKY TRIGGERS: WHAT'S STEALING YOUR PEACE?

"Casting all your anxieties on him, because he cares for you." (1 Peter 5:7 NIV)

Ask yourself this question. How is stress/anxiety/worry affecting your life? The lives of those you love and care about?

Do you want it to change? Do you want to thrive?

Do you tell yourself you aren't stressed and yet your blood pressure is high, you're always on edge, you snap at people, or maybe you drink too much, trying to mask the issues at hand?

Do you wish you could control the feeling of stress in your life? Do you wish you didn't experience anxiety in the middle of the night? Or even driving in the car?

Have you said "Yes" to one or more of these questions?

The dictionary defines *stress* as a "condition typically characterized by symptoms of mental or physical tension or strain, as depression or hypertension, that can result from a *reaction* to a situation in which a person feels threatened, pressured, etc."

Some synonyms for stress are anxiety, nervousness, fearfulness, fear, and tenseness. Some emotional signs or symptoms of stress would be depression, unhappiness, agitation, feeling overwhelmed and lonely.

How often do we say we aren't stressed and yet we feel those emotions I mentioned above?

It just blows my mind that 85% of the things we worry about actually never even happen.

This was crazy to learn. 75-90% of emergency hospital visits, the underlying cause is stress.

Stress is a factor in five out of six leading causes of death; heart disease, cancer, stroke, lower respiratory disease, and accidents.

Have you ever known anyone that has gone to the ER, or the doctor, thinking for sure they were having a heart attack, or maybe they were experiencing high blood pressure, only to be told they were "stressed"? Or maybe they experience anxiety.

I have, several times, and yet often people don't want to admit they are living in a stressed state.

I know back when I was having all my health issues, I sure didn't want to admit I was "stressed", or "worried". Or that I have experienced anxiety, finding myself on the floor crying, hardly able to breathe.

Awareness, and admitting we are stressed or have had anxiety, rather than denial, is the first step in overcoming this in our lives.

It is possible to live in a calmer state.

Dr. Caroline Leaf shares in her book, "Switch on Your Brain", that mind controls matter. If we get this right, we have enormous potential to reach peak health. If we get it wrong, we will be our own worst enemies.

While tightness and constriction in your body can literally be a pain, those feelings can also be instructive. Physical tightness is often a symptom of something going on in our minds. Over the course of our lives, we tend to develop patterns of physical tension in response to stress and difficult emotions. If you can learn to recognize the patterns and correlations between your mind and body, you can intentionally relax those parts of the body before the tension builds.

We can bring negative thoughts to the future, such as "I am so anxious about this or that…" or we can bring positive. I remember preparing to speak at the Women Leaders in Law Enforcement conference in 2019 where 1,100 women police officers were going to be, and I told a friend I was anxious…and she said, "Instead say, I am excited!" I started doing that weeks ahead, and I was not anxious on the day of the event…I was EXCITED!!

Years ago, I was in Southern California, and I knew that the next day I was going to be driving home to the Central Valley. That typically is a six hour drive. I made a comment to a friend and said, " I am dreading tomorrow's drive…" And she said, "How do you know that? It's not tomorrow…"

And she was so right. Why in the world was I so worried about having potential traffic? True I had experienced traffic in the past, many times, and yet that didn't mean it happens every single time.

I will never forget the next day getting up and leaving for home, looking forward to my drive so I could listen to my favorite podcasts, or my favorite music, and my focus became that instead of the traffic.

I sailed right through without traffic. And had there been

some, my mindset had shifted and I was in a completely different space to face it.

Of course, life will never be perfect. We will face hard stuff, we will have traffic, we will have idiots cut us off on the freeway, but the difference will be, we can learn how to respond differently.

Have you ever found yourself all worked up over the "What ifs?"

Well, what if this happens? But what if it doesn't? Here's your reminder…there is an 85% chance it won't.

Think about your own life. How often have you worried about something that never happened?

I love what I heard at church one time that worry doesn't take away tomorrow's troubles, but it does take away today's peace.

More than ever people are experiencing anxiety. A recent study on anxiety in America shows that 32.3% of Americans reported anxiety and depression symptoms in 2023.

Anxiety can hold a tight grip on a person. When we learn to let go of the struggle of anxiety, it can be a powerful antidote to the misery caused by endless unsuccessful struggles with people's emotional pain.

I spoke with another coach recently who has been practicing for over 20 years, and she mentioned she had never seen the rise in anxiety she is seeing now. As explained before, what we experience can be looked at as learning, allowing you to address what is really happening so you can then learn to transform your relationship with anxiety.

I like the saying, "Life is not happening TO YOU, but FOR YOU". That can often be hard to hear, and yet, awareness, even in how it plays out in your body, can be a time for healing.

Another experience that comes to my mind as I write about anxiety and the mind, is when I was in San Diego doing some coaching training for a week. This was during a chapter of my life when my daughter was experiencing some hard stuff. Prior to going I had been having lots of hot flashes and just assumed they were from my age and the hormonal changes I was experiencing. Was it a symptom of perimenopause?

I don't know if you have experienced hot flashes, friend, but they are horrible. I was not just having them during the night, but also often during the day. And here I was in San Diego, almost a week had gone by, and I realized I hadn't had a single one. One day towards the end of the week, my husband called and updated me on a few things happening at home, and I immediately had a hot flash. I will never forget that moment, as I overlooked the ocean from our Airbnb rental, when it dawned on me that some of my hot flashes were actually coming from stress and anxiety of dealing with some of the experiences my daughter was going through at the time.

It wasn't her fault. It was just how my body was reacting.

When I realized that, in a strange way it was comforting. I knew that I would have to figure out a way to look at these life experiences differently, so I could feel better even emotionally. I began to realize I needed to be aware and utilize the tools I was learning that would help me to respond to life versus react.

And it began to help. It's so interesting, because even now, every once in a while, I will begin to have a few hot flashes here and there, waking with them during the night, or even throughout the day, and I will stop and think about it and realize that I am subconsciously worked up over something and it's affecting my body.

It often helps my clients when they realize that anxiety and fear are emotions, not disorders. We've all experienced a certain amount of fear and anxiety in our lives. Some medical professionals use "labels" to describe different forms of human suffering and disease, but I encourage you to remember that labels are not you. If you have experienced anxiety, don't cling to that. It's ok, you are not alone. Focus instead on expanding your life in healthy ways so that you can begin to live a life of more joy and peace.

Think about a time when you were really stressed or anxious...how did you react?

Knowing what you know now, how would you respond differently?

I often speak about "Healthy Habits". Here are 12 Habits that Make Anxiety WORSE. In the second section of this book I will go deeper on the "Healthy Habits" that have helped me live a healthier life, physically, emotionally, spiritually.

1. Drinking too much caffeine. It typically won't affect you right away, and yet is often known as an anxiety amplifier.

2. Skipping Meals. This can lead to hypoglycemia which then can cause irritability, nervousness, dizziness, weakness.

3. Poor Eating Habits. This can affect your intake of essential nutrients that are necessary for our mental health.

4. Not exercising. Our bodies are meant to move, so when we don't it often will make our anxiety worse.

5. Reaching for Sugar. It might feel like it helps at first, and yet studies show that too much sugar increases anxiety and depression. And it affects our ability to sleep.

6. Watching the News. This often leads to a feeling of fear when we are consumed by the negative news, making us feel anxious. Once again, what we focus on, expands.

7. Eating processed foods. There are ingredients in these foods that actually are known to increase anxiety.

8. Not drinking enough water. When we get dehydrated, it causes our bodies to feel stressed which then leads to feelings of

anxiety. (Be sure and read the second half of this book on my "Healthy Habits" where I share more on this subject.)

9. Consuming too much alcohol. It might make you feel relaxed at first, and yet within a few hours of drinking alcohol you will feel worse.

10. Not sleeping enough. When we are tired, our thoughts run rampant, and then it is harder to let go of negative stuff which then increases our anxiety.

11. Comparing ourselves to others. This only causes unhappiness, low mood, and negative thoughts.

12. Ignoring your anxiety. We must be aware. It's ok. And when we address it, we can learn tools to lessen how we are feeling.

Friend, I don't write this from a place of having this all figured out. I am continuously learning from life. We all are.

I truly don't believe this is a one and done learning.

I still have days of feeling anxious. I will notice times when I am easily triggered by something that causes me to head back down the rabbit hole. I occasionally have nights when I lay wide awake thinking about all the things that are out of my control and that will probably never happen.

Thankfully it is way less often than it used to be before I learned these tools I am sharing with you.

Let me share an experience I had.

A COUPLE YEARS AGO, I went to see the podiatrist, and as I sat in the waiting room, a feeling of anxiousness came over me.

(I was being seen for my Plantar Fasciitis and ended up getting some cortisone shots in my heels so I would be able to walk a lot on a trip we took to the East Coast.)

It wasn't because I was nervous about meeting Dr. Tullis,

because I already knew him from the years he helped our daughter Brooke with her rare foot disorder, Tarsal Coalition.

You see, for many years I knew something was not right about Brooke's feet. Even as a three-year-old, she would complain that her feet hurt. I even took her to the Children's Hospital that year, which took eight weeks to even be seen, only to have them tell me nothing was wrong with her feet, and I should just go buy her Stride Rite shoes. Are you kidding me?

In school the teachers would send notes home or even put it on her report cards that she needed to run faster in PE class.

She and I would do yoga together and when I would do the downward dog and my feet were straight behind me, almost touching the ground, hers were turned outward.

Then in eighth grade, it all began to become clearer.

She was walking into an assembly at school when the big heavy metal door slammed right on her foot (miraculously on the exact spot that had the Tarsal Coalition).

She was in pain, she couldn't walk on her foot, so I took her to a local doctor who took an X-ray and told us it wasn't broken, probably just sprained and she could wear this walking boot for support and in no time be better.

Months later, she was still in the boot. And that doctor, told me on a visit, that my daughter should put her foot down and start walking.

I remember being pretty irritated that day and I left that doctor's office and never went back. I felt like he was saying that my daughter's pain was all in her head.

I researched and found a specialist who thankfully was smart enough to do a MRI. Turns out the Tarsal Coalition only shows up on MRIs, and not on X-rays or CT Scans.

Months later we had a diagnosis, and she could have surgery for her rare condition.

Fast forward here…

She had surgery on that foot, followed by one on the other foot, because well, if it's in one, there's a 90% chance it's in the other, followed by having the first foot redone because the bone had grown back where it didn't belong. So, a total of four foot surgeries, followed by casts, boots, crutches, wheelchairs, pain medications, anxiety, and depression.

So, here I am years later, standing at the counter, checking in for my own appointment, and I am triggered.

It all comes flooding back to me. I felt panicky. I can remember taking her picture years ago in the same area I was standing at that exact moment, she has another boot on, because she's just been told that she not only had one Tarsal Coalition in her right foot, but she was even more rare and had two.

And the doctor had never seen this before. There was no way, as a mom, that I was going to allow this doctor to do surgery if he had no idea how to do it. I kindly told our doctor that day that I appreciated him but that we were going to have to research and find someone who felt more confident in having a positive outcome that would allow her to walk and live a life with minimal to no pain.

I hurt for her. I see the pain she is feeling, not just the physical, and yet the fear of not wanting to go through the surgeries again, nor the depression. My heart hurt thinking of all she would potentially have to go through. Again.

I stood there in line that day for my own appointment, feeling anxious, seeing how difficult experiences can trigger us, reminding myself to remember, and to focus on her outcome of how far she has come instead of the negative feelings we had experienced while she was in the midst of this painful chapter of her life.

Certain triggers from past experiences can make us experience anxiety all over again because of how our brain processes and stores emotional memories.

If a past event caused significant stress or trauma, the brain associates similar situations with danger. For example, if someone experienced betrayal in a past relationship, seeing or hearing something related to that person might bring up anxiety, even if no real threat exists at the moment.

The good news? We can rewire our response by becoming aware of triggers, processing past emotions, and practicing new coping mechanisms (such as mindfulness, deep breathing, or reframing our thoughts). Healing is possible!

Thankfully, Brooke's story and this chapter of her life have had a great ending. With the care of the incredible doctors at UCSF, she is now able to walk most days without pain—something we once weren't sure would be possible. Beyond her own healing, she became an advocate for some other young kids and teens around the world who share her diagnosis.

Looking back, I see so clearly how those incredibly difficult days—days filled with uncertainty, fear, and exhaustion—were shaping something far greater than we could have imagined at the time. What felt like an endless storm was, in reality, a season of deep growth. Through it all, Brooke grew closer to God, learning to lean on His strength in every area of her life. Watching her faith flourish in the face of the difficulties has been one of the greatest answers to prayer.

And it didn't just change her—it changed me.

I've learned that trials will come, and suffering is often unavoidable. But we do have a choice in how we respond. Will we allow life's hardships to chain us down, keeping us stuck in fear, resentment, or despair? Or will we choose to release those burdens into the hands of the One who can truly carry them?

Thank God, we don't have to carry them alone. He is always

near, ready to lift our burdens, to redeem our pain, and to turn our struggles into testimonies of His faithfulness. When we surrender to Him, we don't just survive our hardships—we emerge stronger, transformed, and equipped to help others along the way.

HERE ARE **three journal prompts to help you reflect on the ideas in this chapter:**

1. **Identifying Your Triggers:** Think about a recent moment when you felt your body reacting to stress—maybe your heart raced, your shoulders tensed, or you felt overwhelmed. What were you doing or thinking at that moment? Write about any specific situations, thoughts, or memories that seem to trigger your anxiety. How can you start recognizing these triggers earlier?
2. **Shifting Your Mindset:** Reflect on a time when you turned a stressful situation into a positive experience—like changing "I'm dreading this drive" to "I'm excited to listen to my favorite podcast." What did you do differently that day? How did reframing your thoughts affect your emotions and physical state? List some strategies you can use when you feel stress creeping in.
3. **Trusting and Letting Go:** Consider the promise of 1 Peter 5:7: "Casting all your anxieties on him, because he cares for you." Write about a time when you experienced relief after choosing to let go of your worries and trust that someone or something was taking care of you. How did that trust change your

experience of stress, and what steps can you take to lean into that trust more often?

These prompts are designed to help you uncover your stress triggers, explore ways to shift your mindset, and deepen your trust in a power that cares for you. Enjoy your reflection!

CHAPTER 5
THE TRAP OF DOING: WHY PEACE COMES FROM BEING

"Seek the Kingdom of God, above all else, and live righteously, and he will give you everything you need." (Matt. 6:33 New Living Translation)

A favorite quote of mine, by Wayne Dyer is, "We don't attract what we want, we attract who we are."

Years ago, I was taking a week of coach training in San Diego.

I was sitting in the class when this concept I am going to share was taught to me.

It was life changing for me.

Have you ever heard of the BE DO HAVE CONCEPT?

Most people believe that once they HAVE more money in the bank, more credentials, degrees, a new spouse, and better looks, once they get healthier, they will be able to DO whatever they want.

And only then can they become happy, confident, and fulfilled.

Most people operate in a Have-Do-Be mindset, believing that once they have something (money, time, confidence), they can do what they need to, and then they will be happy, successful, or fulfilled.

This often leads to frustration and a cycle of waiting for external conditions to change before we take action.

Years ago, I was totally living this. I, too, was sure that everything would be better if I had more money, the debt was paid off and I had a different career.

Hey, when I started on this journey of transformation, (remember, the shower story a couple chapters ago?), financially we were struggling, the economy was tight, and we owed more on our house than it was worth. Life was hard.

I could've used that situation as an excuse even for not working on my health.

I couldn't afford a gym membership then, but I could walk; that was free. And so, I walked miles a day. And I found some really great workouts on YOUTUBE that were free as well.

I realized I had been living all this backwards. It wasn't about HAVE DO BE, but rather BE DO HAVE.

You must become first in order to do what is necessary so you can have what you want.

How does this work?

INSTEAD OF WAITING for circumstances to change, we start with who we are:

1. **BE** – Decide the kind of person you need to be. What mindset, beliefs, and identity align with your goals? Do you need to be confident, disciplined, faithful, peaceful?

2. **DO** – Take action from that identity. If you are already "being" that person, what habits, choices, and behaviors naturally follow?
3. **HAVE** – As a result of being and doing, you naturally attract and achieve what you desire.

Instead of thinking, "Once I have more time, I will work on my health, and then I will be confident,"

- Shift to: "I am a person who values my health (BE), so I make time to move my body and nourish it (DO), and as a result, I have energy and confidence (HAVE)."

Instead of "Once I have financial security, I will give more and be generous,"

- Shift to "I am already a generous person (BE), so I look for ways to give, even in small ways (DO), and abundance follows (HAVE)."

Why does this work?

- It aligns with biblical principles of faith and identity: "As a man thinks in his heart, so is he" (Proverbs 23:7).
- It shifts your focus from external conditions to internal transformation.
- It creates momentum, because instead of waiting for circumstances to change, you step into your future self NOW.

Ask yourself this question, Are you BEING who you need to be in order to create the things you want to HAVE?

After that training, I began telling myself, "I AM a loving, compassionate, inspiring soul." I personally chose soul because I am a Christian and I knew that SOUL pretty much could encompass every part of my life. A mom, a wife, a life coach, a friend, all the things.

But maybe you're a teacher and you want to have a better-paying position, or you're a business owner and you just want to have more money coming in.

And you find yourself always focusing on the doing. And yet you begin each day feeling frustrated, irritated, and doubtful, you talk to yourself, "Like I will never have this or that…"

How can you apply this to your life?

1. Identify a goal or desire.
2. Ask yourself: Who do I need to be to achieve this?
3. Start embodying that identity with small actions (DO).
4. Trust that the results (HAVE) will come naturally.

HEALTH & FITNESS EXAMPLE

Maybe you're struggling with fitness and weight loss goals. To achieve lasting results, you first have to **BE** someone who chooses healthier ways to manage stress—rather than turning to comfort eating or skipping workouts. It means **BEing** willing to let go of what's sabotaging your progress. (For me, it was carbs. I wasn't just eating one Ritz cracker, I was finishing the whole sleeve!)

Once you shift your mindset, you start to **DO** the things that align with your new identity, like saying no to that second slice of cake and committing to a 30-minute workout. And the result? You **HAVE** the wellness and health you've been striving for.

BUSINESS & SALES EXAMPLE

If you're a business owner looking to grow your sales, you must first **BE** someone who confidently promotes their service or product. That shift in identity leads to **DOing** what it takes—showing up, marketing, and making offers—which ultimately allows you to **HAVE** the increased sales and success you desire.

OVERCOMING OVERWHELM AS AN ENTREPRENEUR

Many of you are entrepreneurs who feel overwhelmed by the sheer number of tasks on your plate. You know you need help, yet you struggle to let go and trust others. In this case, success requires you to **BE** someone who is willing to delegate. As you step into that mindset, you begin to **DO** what's necessary—handing off tasks, trusting others with their strengths—and in return, you **HAVE** more time, balance, and growth in your business.

The key is to stop waiting for the outcome before changing your mindset. Instead, start by **BEing** the person who aligns with the life you want, and watch how your actions and results follow.

This was totally me. I was afraid back when I first started my Life Coaching practice, I was a new business owner. How could I possibly hire someone to help me do the tasks that maybe I personally wasn't that great at, it wasn't my strong point. How was I going to afford it?

I often felt like I was spinning my wheels because I was trying to do all the things myself. I would waste so much time on something a social media person could do in minutes. If I could hire them, I would have less stress.

Fortunately for me, I was able to barter some of my to-dos at first until I could hire some of it out.

Have you felt that way? As a business owner I had to get to the place where I let go of my ego, recognized that I had to invest in my business and hire out some of what was holding me back.

This stuff doesn't just happen, it's a choice. It's a mindset.

And guess what? It can be learned. It's a continuous process. I did it, and you can, too.

START BEING THAT PERSON NOW. Don't wait.

A Major part of the word "BE" is our thoughts. If you want different results, you must begin to DO something different, even in how you think and talk to yourself.

I love what Ed Mylett shares in his book The Power of One More, "Your thoughts and your actions must be congruent".

God can't steer a parked car. I have no idea where I heard that one time, but it is so true, isn't it? We can't just sit around expecting things to happen. It does not work that way.

Have you ever tried to steer a parked car? It's impossible. The car has to be moving in order for the power steering to work. The wheel won't turn to the left or the right. You will stay stuck right where you are. And you won't be able to move forward.

Do you want to see change in your life? Then it begins with taking that first step. Decide who you will BE, and then you will start moving in the right direction that God is leading you. Let him direct you.

Another favorite verse is "The Lord directs the steps of the godly. He delights in every detail of their lives." (Ps. 37:23 NLT)

When you take the first step, God's "Power steering" will kick in. And you will start seeing that he directs your next step, and the next one, and the next one. (Proverbs 16:9) Let him direct you.

We first figure out who we want to BE, what our values are, what is most important to us, and then we follow that up with the DOING that then leads to the HAVING, the results.

Did you see that? We BE first and then we want to DO.

As it pertains to our spiritual life, we can easily get caught up in attempting to get right with God through all we are DOING. Through works. How much can I do? Is it by showing up to church every week, (although fellowship is wonderful) or being involved and volunteering for all the things?

A verse that has really opened up to me is in Ephesians 2:8-10. "God saved you by his grace when you believed. And you can't take any credit for this; it is a gift from God. Salvation is not a reward for the good things we have done, so none of us can boast about it. For we are God's masterpiece. He has created us anew in Christ Jesus, so we can do the good things he planned for us long ago.

And one day you will eventually arrive at the destination where he is leading you."

We want to *DO* because we are saved by grace. Not because of anything we did. It's nothing of ourselves that saves us.

BUT HOW DO I DO THIS DARLA?

I want to encourage you to create your own "BE" statement that can be life changing for you.

Here is how to do this:
1. Reflect on Who You Want to Become
Ask yourself:

- What kind of person do I want to **BE** in my daily life?
- How do I want others to experience me?
- If I were already living my best, most aligned life, how would I describe myself?

Example Prompts:

- I want to be someone who _____ (shows up with confidence, walks in peace, loves without fear, takes bold action, etc.).
- When people think of me, I want them to describe me as _____ (kind, strong, faithful, joyful, wise, courageous, etc.).

2. Choose 3-5 Core Words

Choose a few words that resonate with the person you want to become. These words should inspire you and remind you of your highest self.

Example Words:

- **Faith-based**: Faithful, Grace-filled, Obedient, Trusting, Prayerful
- **Character-focused**: Compassionate, Confident, Joyful, Wise, Loving
- **Purpose-driven**: Disciplined, Fearless, Impactful, Radiant, Aligned

3. Turn It Into a Simple, Powerful "I AM" Statement

Once you have your words, begin to form your personal **BE** statement. It should be present-tense, empowering, and something you can affirm daily.

Examples:

- I am a bold, faith-filled woman who trusts God's plan.
- I am a joyful, peaceful, and purpose-driven soul.
- I am a confident, radiant, and inspiring leader.
- I am a compassionate, wise, and deeply loving person.

4. Make It a Daily Affirmation

I encourage you to say your BE statement out loud every morning, write it in a journal, or place it somewhere you will see it daily. This reinforces the identity shift.

What helped me as I began implementing this into my own life was I wrote it on sticky notes and I had one on my laptop, and another on my car dash so I could see it every day.

I will tell you; it took some time for me to begin seeing the changes of me living into "I am a loving, compassionate, inspiring soul".

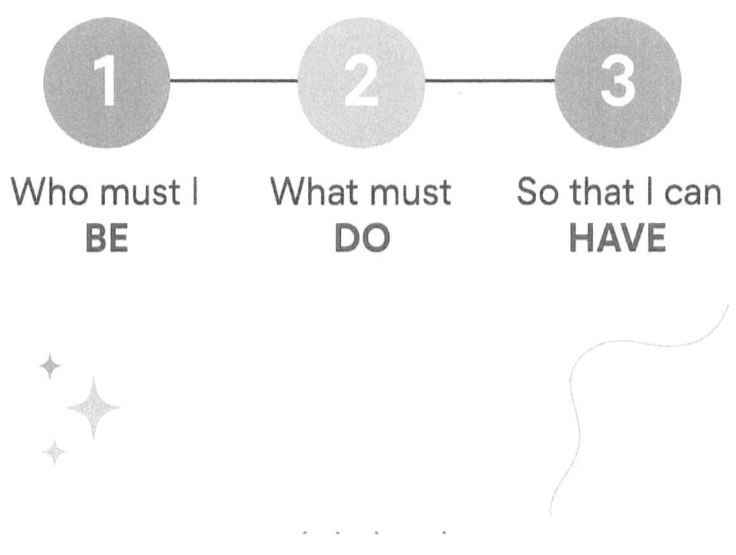

Maybe yours is, I am a confident, happy, encouraging mom, dad, teacher, real estate agent, contractor, _____ you fill in the blank…

REMEMBER, we don't attract what we want, we attract who we are.

No one wants to BE a lazy, never on time person.

Or an angry, frustrated employee.

If you are those things, if you live into being those things, you will continue to be them.

Do you see how thinking that could help you in your day? Versus maybe starting with, "I'm a horrible mom, I'm never going to get that raise, I will never have money in my savings."

When I started changing my way of BEING, opportunities started happening, clients started coming to me instead of me chasing them.

I also started to feel more joy in my life. More peace.

I remember one day sitting at my desk, working, trying to create programs and do the best I could for my clients so they would get results. I was discouraged. I was tired.

I had the saying, "I am a loving, compassionate, inspiring soul" on a sticky note on my laptop. I found myself yelling it to myself. I wasn't believing it. Tears came. Frustration came. I wanted to quit.

I love that God can help us with who we are meant to be. He can help me redirect my thoughts to Him and what truly matters.

I used to be so focused on how many clients I was supposed to have, how much I was supposed to charge, how was I going to update my website and funnels when I didn't know how, or have the time. I would be filled with anxious thoughts. I would feel overwhelmed.

I still think it's a bit comical that I used to have such a negative money mindset being that I had been a financial advisor for years.

Things began to shift when I lived into the person I felt I was called to be.

By changing my way of BEING, I even got healthier, not just physically, but mentally, too. My way of being inspired me to exercise, drink my water, and see the good in others. I learned the importance of living out what I refer to as my "Happy Healthy Habits".

You picked up this book for a reason. You want things to be different. In life, in business, in relationships.

By being secure in who you are being, even when hard things happen, you will continue to live into your values. You will be the same person at home, at work, at church, and all the places.

Living by the Be-Do-Have concept is one of the most powerful shifts you can make. Instead of waiting for circumstances to change, you become the kind of person who creates the life you desire.

No more waiting. No more hoping things will get better "someday."

When you **BE** the person who is confident, disciplined, loving, or faith-filled, you naturally begin to **DO** the things that align with that identity—leading you to **HAVE** the results you once only dreamed of.

How This Changes Everything

- **You step into your purpose NOW.** Instead of waiting until you feel ready, you start showing up as the person you are meant to be.
- **You gain confidence.** No longer held back by fear or self-doubt, you take action from a place of certainty.
- **You attract the right opportunities.** When you operate as the person you aspire to be, doors begin to open.

◆ **You stop living in frustration.** Instead of thinking, "If only I had more time, money, energy…" you shift to "I am capable, resourceful, and equipped now."

◆ **You experience more peace and joy.** When your identity aligns with your goals, there's no more inner conflict—just flow.

Imagine this:

- Instead of saying, *"I'll be happy when I lose weight,"* you decide, *"I am a healthy and strong person,"* and you will see that making better choices becomes easier.
- Instead of saying, *"I'll feel secure when I have more money,"* you shift to, *"I am a wise steward of my finances,"* and you begin handling money differently.
- Instead of saying, *"I'll be successful when I have more clients,"* you affirm, *"I am a confident business owner,"* and you start showing up in a way that attracts people to you.

YOUR LIFE WILL CHANGE WHEN YOU DO

This shift doesn't happen overnight, but when you commit to **BEing** first, you'll notice small transformations adding up to a completely new way of living.

♡ **So today, I challenge you:** Step into the person God created you to be. Act as if you already are that person, because the truth is—you are! And as you live in that truth, you'll see your life align with the desires of your heart.

You've got this! I believe in YOU.

With God, all is possible.

How we perceive ourselves emerges from our doing, and our habits.

I know your life will change when you begin to live into this.

Maybe in the past you would have blown up, given up, and now you can see that it's just a fork in the road, or one small step backwards.

It takes time to unlearn the things we have always done, it takes time to learn how to respond versus react and to learn new concepts, new perspectives, so be patient. Allow yourself grace. Pray for help.

I love knowing that God cares about every single part of our lives.

Friend, you will begin to acknowledge your emotions, your feelings, instead of hiding them, or avoiding them.

And you will be so glad you did the work. I am here to help you every step of the way because I care.

Here are three journal prompts to help you dive deeper into the "BE DO HAVE" concept and explore the shift from doing to being:

1. **Reflect on Your Past "Doing" Mindset:** Think back to a time when you believed that having more—whether it was money, success, or a specific outcome—would make you happy. What was the gap between that belief and the reality you experienced? How did focusing on doing rather than being impact your peace and fulfillment?
2. **Create Your "BE" Statement:** Consider the qualities you admire most in people who live with confidence, joy, and purpose. What are 3-5 core words that describe the person you want to be? Write a personal "I AM" statement (for example, "I am a compassionate, resilient, and faith-filled soul"). How

can you start embodying this identity today in your daily actions?
3. **Shift in Action, Shift in Results:** Reflect on a situation where changing your mindset (from "I will be happy when..." to "I am..."), helped you take actions that aligned with your true self. What specific changes did you notice in your behavior, relationships, or outcomes? How might living more into your future self help you create the life you desire?

These prompts are designed to help you explore how transforming your inner identity can create a ripple effect in your actions and ultimately lead to the peace and fulfillment you seek. Enjoy the reflection!

CHAPTER 6
WORDS THAT HEAL, WORDS THAT HARM: USING YOUR VOICE FOR GOOD

"Do not use foul or abusive language. Let everything you say be good and helpful, so that your words will be an encouragement to those who hear them." (Eph. 4:29 translation)

As I continued on this journey of really learning more about our thoughts, how we think and how we talk to ourselves, I became enthralled with the power that there is in the words we speak.

The words we speak to ourselves and to others. The words we think and maybe don't even audibly say.

I began studying this concept and realized that this is often a missing link for people.

Do you believe that the words you speak create the life you live?

Let's think about this for a moment.

I want you to think about how you talk to yourself, whether internally in your mind or to others. Have you been telling yourself or others in your life that you will never find a spouse, that you are unsuccessful, miserable, bored, fat, or whatever else it is that you have been saying?

The words you speak—both out loud and in your thoughts—hold incredible power. Every time you say something, you are reinforcing a belief, setting an intention, and influencing your energy. Whether you realize it or not, your words are shaping your reality.

That is not fun to hear, I know. But it is true.

When you say something out loud enough times, your words become the truth, not just to yourself, but even people around you begin believing it.

Some of us know this instinctively, while others come to this understanding slowly. Most of us, though, speak without thinking at least some of the time, blurting out our feelings and thoughts without much regard for the words we choose to express them. Your mind is always listening.

Negative Words Keep You Stuck:

- "I'm so overwhelmed." → Reinforces stress.
- "I'll never get this right." → Lowers confidence.
- "I'm not good enough." → Creates self-doubt.

Positive Words Shift Your Energy:

- "I am capable and resourceful." → Increases confidence.
- "I choose peace at this moment." → Lowers stress.
- "I am growing and learning every day." → Encourages resilience.

THE BIBLE REMINDS us of this truth: "The tongue has the power of life and death." (Prov. 18:21)

What you speak brings either life or limitation. Speaking words of faith, hope, and truth aligns your energy with the life you desire.

I read recently that we can either make beautiful music with the words we speak or we run the risk of creating a noisy disturbance.

When I think of words, and scripture there are some hard truths to pay attention to.

One of which is that God holds us responsible for our words. Our words can create a significant impact. Imagine a ship rudder steering a large boat, our tongue has the ability to have a very big impact. For good or bad.

Or imagine the tongue being like a wild animal with the ability to tear someone apart.

I think one of the most detrimental results of words is how they can potentially influence a relationship.

And yet it doesn't have to be that way. We can learn to pay attention to how we speak, the words we say, and the spirit in which we say them.

Are you even aware of how you are talking to yourself? Do you realize the impact it can have on your life?

How many of you are familiar with NEUROPLASTICITY? One of my favorite books I referred to before is called "Switch on Your Brain" by Dr. Caroline Leaf, and in it, she teaches that our brains can actually change and grow.

If you are apt to think thoughts such as:

- Someone else can do this better than me.
- I will never break free from this.

The cool thing is our brains have the neuroplasticity, or the ability, to redirect those negative trains of thought.

This will take time and practice as well as a desire for change. In the midst of learning how to do this we experience discomfort in growth, but this practice can ultimately change so much of your life.

We aren't born with a negative mindset; it's something we acquire through life's experiences. And yet, we have the ability to change it and create a new reality for ourselves!

WE CAN LEARN to USE WORDS as tools. If you choose the right words, you begin to see how they are helping you have better relationships and a better life. To have a mind full of peace, it takes practice.

I loved hearing this years ago: talk peacefully to be peaceful.

I don't remember where I read this, but I loved it. "We can choose to use our **words** for encouragement, or destructively using **words** of despair. **Words** have energy and **power** with the ability to help, to heal, to hinder, to hurt, to harm, to humiliate, and to humble."

We must start filling our minds with creative and healthy thoughts. The old fears, hates, and worries that haunt us from our past, will often try to edge their way back in, and they will try to stay. We must remember that how we used to think and talk doesn't just magically disappear overnight. And yet, the new and healthy thoughts which you have taken in will now become stronger and you can repulse the negative ones."

People often don't realize that words have the power to keep them from the success they are striving for. I love watching people transform their lives when they are able to let go of words that have held them back and they can do so without shaming and blaming others. Even the words they told themselves.

Do this exercise:

Let's FEEL the difference.

Try it, Say the word HATE.

HOW DOES THAT FEEL?

Then say the word LOVE,

How do you feel?

Can you FEEL THE DIFFERENCE?

Even the energy of those words is different.

See the power in those words?

A few weeks ago, I got a call from a client who was sobbing. She had had a challenging experience a few days prior, a trigger from a horrible time in her past had just happened, and now a few days later she was in complete anxiety mode. She was telling herself, "I have so much anxiety, I can hardly breathe".

Knowing where this anxiety was coming from, I had to ask her questions to help her see that by telling herself over and over, "I have so much anxiety, I can't breathe", she truly was getting more of it.

Instead, I asked her, "That experience you had last week, have you had it before?" No. Have you been to hundreds of clients' homes and felt safe? Yes. What can you say differently? Think differently? She started to say, "I have the tools to help me on this journey of wellness", and "God has helped me overcome this before, he will provide again". And so on. Within five minutes of us talking, I could hear her breathing change, she was calmer and she was able to continue on to her next client's appointment.

Our words reinforce either a positive or a negative perspective. Our words, subtly, echo the story we tell ourselves every single day. A story that after a while becomes what we tend to believe.

What we don't realize is that words we are often habitually saying are energetically affecting our lives.

In "The Mountain is You", by Brianna Wiest, she says that we have a lot of language that clues us into where we have physical reactions to emotions. We often feel fear in our stomachs (think of a nervous stomach, or a gut instinct) and heartache in our chests (that's where the whole broken heart thing comes from), stress and anxiety in our shoulders (think of the weight of the world on your shoulders), and relationship problems in the neck (think they are a pain in the neck).

Do you see now why it's key to speak and think of words that will benefit our health, our life, and our relationships?

Let's look at words you have probably said to yourself...

I'm stupid. I have the worst luck. I'm sloppy. I'm terrible with money. I'm unlovable. I don't have any common sense. I'm a failure.

What if instead, you started asking yourself questions to prove otherwise? Start talking to yourself with love and kindness.

A big awakening too for me was in reading a book called AFFORMATIONS by Noah St. John.

I love how he teaches this concept just a little bit differently.

Our brains, when asked the right questions, will search until it finds the answers.

So, instead of *"Why am I so stupid?"*, say, *"Why do I educate myself until I find the answers?"*

Or, instead of *"Why am I terrible with money?"*, say, *"Why do I believe that I will be successful and that my income will increase?"*

When I read his book and started applying it, wow, I saw a difference in how I felt about my life, my business, my relationships.

Noah St. John teaches that when we ask the right questions, our brain will start answering the questions. Just as when we make a negative statement or ask a negative question, our brain looks for validation as to why it's true, so is it true when we ask the right questions.

We must begin to ask ourselves the right questions.

I love how he explained why he feels it's important to ask "why" questions. He says, "Two basic forces govern human behavior: the why and the how. The **why** is your motive for doing something. The **how** is your method of doing it.

I think it's so true when he explains that we often know how to do something, but we just don't. Motive always trumps method.

We also can get into the habit of saying certain words without realizing it, never considering the impact it is having on our life.

I was talking to someone a while back and I began to notice how often she said, "I have to do this," and "I have to do that." As her words became more obvious, I realized how many times she said it in that one conversation we were having. I set out on my own experiment of consciously listening to how many times I would naturally say "have to" in a conversation as well as how many times others would. It was much more than I expected. You should try this experiment yourself.

It was a subtle thing, an unconscious word choice, but a choice all the same.

It was really eye opening for me to pay attention to myself and how often I was using those words, too.

HAVE TO frames things in a way that says I am obligated or required. It's negative in most cases.

GET TO frames it more from a sense of gratitude and appreciation. It's positive.

Do you notice the difference? It's a simple shift of perspective but it can mean a lot over time as we begin to train our brains to respond out of a place of gratitude and thanksgiving versus obligation.

The truth is, there's not much in life we *have to* do but there is a lot in life we *get to* do.

1. That job that you *have to* go to each day, yeah, you get to go, you get to earn a paycheck regardless of how small or large it may be.
2. That meeting you *have to* go to, yeah…you get to go there, too. Could be worse, you could be sick or injured and physically not able to.
3. That bill you *have to* pay, again…you get to.

This was a big shift for me. Years ago, we had a lot of medical debt after my daughter had four surgeries. We hadn't previously gone to the doctor much, so we had insurance with a large deductible to keep our premiums lower. After her surgeries were over, we still owed over $20,000 dollars. Every month I would get in a bad mood while paying them, until one day it dawned on me that maybe I needed to start looking at it differently.

I started saying to myself, I *get to* pay these bills because, without them, my daughter wouldn't be walking. Because of those surgeries, the doctors fixed her rare foot disorder and she went from living a life of pain and restriction to being able to live, walk, and even do simple hikes again.

You can imagine the gratitude I had when I was down to only $3,000 dollars left to pay the surgeon and I called one day to get an updated balance. To my surprise they said they had no record of her bill anymore and that according to their records we had a zero balance!

So, go ahead, make the choice today to replace have to with get to and see how your perspective begins to change.

I dare you to consciously start paying attention to the words you use.

Are there words that you are using that could be hindering your growth? Often words keep us from moving forward and they will keep us stuck.

Another word that people often use is the word hard. Life is hard. Relationships are hard. Work is hard.

During a session with a client, I remember listening to her explain what was going on in her life, about how everything was hard. It seemed like every other word she was speaking was the word "hard". I asked her permission if I could share something I had noticed.

And so I pointed out what my experience had been. She was amazed to realize that this word had become such a part of her vocabulary. It had become a habit.

Using the word hard frequently can hinder our growth because it often carries a negative connotation and can create mental barriers. When we repeatedly describe tasks or challenges as hard, we inadvertently reinforce the idea that they are difficult, which can lead to feelings of discouragement, frustration, or even avoidance.

I am sure I am not the only one who avoids things that are hard to do, right?

Instead of focusing on everything being hard or difficult, we can begin to replace the word hard with maybe a word like challenging, or complex. This shift in our language will then alter our perspective and we will begin to approach challenges with a more positive and moving forward mindset.

What I have noticed for myself is that by changing certain words, like going from hard to challenging, I began to see challenges as opportunities for growth, and it motivated me to persevere and overcome obstacles.

We will all experience challenges and obstacles, my friend. It will come down to how we view them and how we respond to them, as to whether or not we move ahead, or stay stuck.

Nobody should stay stuck. Are you ready to change your words?

Here are three journal prompts to help you reflect on the power of words and how they shape your life:

1. **Reflect on Your Inner Dialogue:** What are some of the recurring phrases or thoughts you tell yourself—both positive and negative? Write them down. Now, choose one negative thought and reframe it into a positive affirmation (for example, turning "I'm not good enough" into "I am capable and growing every day"). How does changing your inner dialogue shift your feelings and actions?
2. **Words in Action:** Think back to a recent conversation or moment when you noticed your words either uplifting or hurting yourself or someone else. What did you say, and how did it make you feel? In hindsight, how might you have chosen different words to create a more healing, encouraging impact? Consider how this change in language could influence your relationships and overall well-being.
3. **From "Have To" to "Get To":** Reflect on an area of your life where you often use the phrase "I have to…" (e.g., "I have to work" or "I have to pay bills"). Now, reframe that thought into "I get to…" (e.g., "I get to work on something I love" or "I get to support my family"). How does this simple shift in language change your perspective about that part of your day or life? What

might this change in perspective do for your stress levels and sense of gratitude?

These prompts are designed to help you explore how your words—both spoken and unspoken—affect your mindset, relationships, and overall energy. Enjoy your reflection!

CHAPTER 7
WORDS THAT HEAL, WORDS THAT HURT

"Gentle words are a tree of life; a deceitful tongue crushes the spirit." (Prov. 15:4 NLT)

Benjamin Franklin once said, "Remember not only to say the right thing, in the right place but far more important still, to leave unsaid the wrong thing at the tempting moment."

As I coach people, I am often told about words that were spoken to someone, that maybe the person speaking them might not even remember, and yet the person hearing them, years, even decades later, still hold on to them.

As words can be used negatively, they can also build someone up and even change their lives, for the better.

It makes me think of over 30 years ago when my brother passed away after years of struggling with brain tumors. I will never forget when he had the first one. I was still in high school. It's always interesting to me the details we remember and those we forget. For some reason, I remember the doctor calling late in the evening to tell us he had a brain tumor. So, then he had surgery. I remember being angry and sad. I remember pounding the wall in the hospital hallway, saying, "Why God, why?" not understanding why my brother had to experience this. I was grateful for my mom who came to me and comforted me and assured me that God would be with me in this experience.

I will never forget going into the recovery room at the hospital as he was coming off the anesthesia. I was holding his hand and talking to him, although he was still not awake. Hoping he would come out of it and still be able to talk, walk, and know us. He squeezed my hand. That was the greatest feeling.

My brother went on to experience several more brain tumors and surgeries to remove them. Every time he had another surgery, we wondered if he would make it. I was married with two young sons at the time, and we lived six hours away from my parents and my brother's family.

I will never forget getting a call in the middle of the night that my brother passed away.

My mom was calling us from Iowa where they were visiting my paternal grandfather because he was failing as well, and my brother wanted to see him before grandpa died. Interestingly enough, my brother died first.

That day still feels so surreal. I can't imagine now, as a mom myself, what my parents were experiencing having just lost their son.

There ended up being a funeral in Iowa with the family there, and then they shipped his body home on the airplane so we could have another funeral in California.

Seeing my brother's body coming off the plane with the luggage felt so wrong.

As I write this, I am realizing again how much this experience affected me. And how much it influenced who I have become today.

Of course, I was sad. I couldn't imagine life without my brother. It felt hard to exist, to be a mom and do all the things we do. Even changing a diaper seemed difficult at the time. How was our family supposed to get through this experience?

And then someone shared some words with me that changed my life.

A dear friend of almost 35 years, called to console me, listened as I cried, and told me to hang up the phone, go in my room, and pray and beg God to help me move on. I did. I begged God to give me strength, to give this very difficult experience to him. And I remember the feeling of peace and comfort that came over me. God had given me strength to get up and do what I needed to do as a mom and a wife.

It wasn't that it became so much easier, of course, I still missed him, but now I had the power of God helping me along.

Years later, this same person experienced something really hard in her life. One day as we visited over lunch, I reminded her of the words she had spoken to me all those years ago, and now I was encouraging her to do the same. I encouraged her to give this very difficult experience to God. To pray about it.

What was amazing, is that I found out from her that she had no recollection of having told me that. She was just being the friend that she is and was speaking from her heart. She had no idea the power of the words she had spoken and how they changed my life.

How was it possible that she didn't even remember having said those words to me? I just love thinking about that again as I write this because God often puts the right people in our lives at the exact moment we need them. It was just evidence to me again that there is power in our words. What we say matters. We can influence others with our words, for good, and we can use hurtful words that people hold onto for a long time.

The way you speak -- the attitude and tone -- reflects the person you are and impacts everything around you. It can greatly contribute to your success or non-success both in business and your personal life.

OUR WORDS BECOME OUR EXPERIENCES. What we say to ourselves, or even to others, whether audible or even in our minds, often becomes our truth.

Please, think before you speak. It will make all the difference.

As I mentioned earlier, our words can help, or they can hinder.

Have you ever been misunderstood? I think we all have. And we have all misunderstood others.

I will tell you about a time over 10 years ago when someone said something to me that crushed me.

I honestly don't think I had ever been spoken to like that before. My heart hurt so much. I cried a lot. For the longest time, I kept this experience to myself and only shared it with my husband. And God.

I knew that hurting people, hurt people. She had just gone through a hard experience, and I guess I was the scapegoat that day.

I prayed earnestly about that experience. For quite a while I was guarded and protected my feelings. I knew I needed coaching on how to handle my heart on this because it often was consuming my thoughts.

Many years later there was an opportunity, a phone call, where I was able to share with this person how those words had hurt that day.

She had no recollection of ever having said what she had. I remember where I was sitting, while on the phone, when she said, "Wow, I said that?" That was when I knew once again, that hurting people, hurt people.

I was thankful in that moment that I had shown her love and grace. That, although very hard, I had prayed for this relationship a lot, knowing that God was also using this experience to show me my own heart. Would I hold a grudge? Would I forgive? This relationship was and is so important to me, that during those first years after this experience, I felt it was eating my heart. I had to surrender this to God. I am grateful I let this go, with the help of God.

I think it is key to remember that often in life we will misunderstand each other. We will say things that hurt. And we will have hurtful things said to us, but how will we respond? How will we react?

IN MY STUDIES of becoming a Certified Life Coach, I learned Neuro Linguistic Programming and a very important concept called the Communication Model.

Learning this helped me to see how important communication is to our relationships.

At any given moment, our brains are bombarded with about **11 million bits** of information per second from our surroundings —what we see, hear, feel, smell, and even remember.

Imagine for a moment that you are listening to me at a conference. The room is full, maybe people are mulling around; someone sneezes or blows their nose. Maybe the person in front of you has a nervous habit of messing with her hair that you can't help but focus on.

And you just are trying to listen to what I am sharing.

What's amazing is that everyone that is listening is going to catch something different. Maybe while listening, you're noticing my dress, or you're staring at the cute guy or gal across the way. Maybe you just remembered something you need to write down about an upcoming appointment. Or maybe, just maybe, you are there in body, and yet you have experienced something really hard, so you truly aren't listening.

We can only consciously process about **134 bits** per second.

Not everyone is catching the same 134 bits per second. Even the person sitting right next to you. Maybe it's your spouse and what he/she heard is different from what you said.

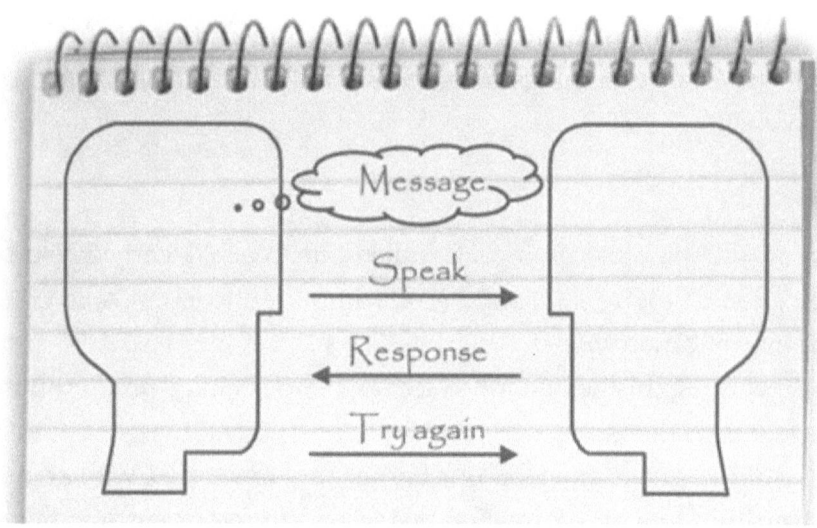

WOULDN'T this help if we learned about this more when we are communicating with our spouses, children, family, coworkers?

Imagine you're at your favorite coffee shop having a conversation with a friend. Here's what's happening:

The **11 million bits** of information from our surroundings might include:

- The smell of coffee
- The sound of espresso machines steaming milk
- Background music playing
- People talking at other tables
- The feeling of the chair under you
- The temperature of your coffee cup
- Your phone buzzing in your pocket
- Your thoughts about your to-do list

The **134 bits** you focus on and process might be:

- Your friend's voice
- Their facial expressions
- The words they're saying

Why does this matter?

This is when misunderstandings happen. If someone is distracted, stressed, or focused on something else, they might miss an important part of what you're saying.

Truly I think this is why intentional communication is so key to every relationship we have.

We live in a time when there are constant bits of information flying at us from everywhere. People often can't put their phones away even during a meal with family or friends.

How often have you noticed in a restaurant, everyone at the

table, together in person, and yet all on their phones. What really saddens my heart, is when I see little kids with their parents, and the mom or dad are always scrolling, looking at their phones, when they could be engaging with their kids.

I've been guilty, too.

The next time you are having a conversation with your spouse, family member, coworker, friend, be present, ask them to be present, and just know, they might not be catching what you hoped they would.

I know it has helped me to have better communication with my spouse. We both have been guilty of having discussions with each other, all the while on our phones, scrolling, reading texts we have received, and we truly aren't hearing each other.

Do you know anyone who might have ADD or ADHD? Or maybe they just have squirrel tendencies. That could totally be me. Without conscious attention, communication can get a little tricky.

"Communication is the response that we get", simply means that when we talk, it's not always understood. It's not determined by what you intend to say, but rather by how the other person understands and reacts to it.

This really helped me because If I am not being understood, could it be that I am not using the right words? Or that they "heard" something different than what I said?

Even more recently, having made a very difficult decision to leave a church, a fellowship that we had attended our entire lives, we encountered a few, (thankfully not many) who have said some really unkind words.

The words stung. And once again, I have had to remind myself that they hurt, too.

It's not easy. Sometimes they come in the form of a text

message. Which personally, I think is not the place for having difficult conversations.

I often wonder if we hide behind text messages. Do we say things in text messages that we would never say in person? I know for some, writing our feelings is easier than verbally expressing them. I get that. And yet, I feel text messages are often misunderstood.

My initial reaction to one of the texts I received was, "WOW". I had to take a deep breath and pray before responding. I always suggest in those instances to ask the person to call you so you can have the conversation on the phone, as you don't ever want to take the chance of having misunderstood their words.

Often, they won't call. It's ok. We are all in different places on our life journey and when we allow ourselves to let it go, we will know more peace.

I had a decision to make after receiving that text. Was I going to allow those words to keep me in a funk and sad, or was I going to make a decision to give those experiences to God and let those words go?

My natural thought was to hold on, but that would just make me feel miserable for longer.

I knew too, that I needed to address my own heart, my own hurt. What was I feeling? Anger, sadness, judgment?

I would know a lot more peace if I was willing to show love and grace to that person. I feel for this person. I love her, I love her soul. I truly care.

I did let it take me down for a bit, and that is ok. God created our emotions, and it is key to allow ourselves to feel the emotions so we can heal from them.

I have brought it to God quite a few times in all transparency.

Now that I think about it, I am glad. It brought me to my knees. A lot.

I had to remind myself that I was focused on the few who had hurt me instead of focusing on the large amount of support we have from many others in our lives.

I wonder how many relationships could be mended if people paid attention to the words they speak. Or even for us to say, "I am sorry", for something we have said that hurt someone else, or that we regret saying and feel really bad about.

We all have done this. We all have said hurtful things, maybe without even realizing it. And I am sure we all have even sent text messages that maybe weren't so nice or were received incorrectly.

Using texting to communicate when you are upset can lead to several negative outcomes. Here are some reasons why I suggest avoiding texting in such situations:

1. **Lack of Non-Verbal Cues**: Texting lacks the non-verbal cues such as tone of voice, facial expressions, and body language that are crucial in conveying emotions and intentions accurately. This can lead to misunderstandings and make the situation not play out as you had hoped.
2. **Impulsivity**: When upset, people tend to react impulsively. Texting makes it easy to send messages without fully thinking through the consequences. These impulsive messages can be hurtful and difficult to take back. This is why I personally believe it is key to take a deep breath and pray before answering a difficult message.
3. **Misinterpretation**: Written words can be easily misinterpreted, especially when emotions are running high. A message meant to express frustration might be

perceived as anger, or a plea for understanding might seem as if you are accusing them.
4. **Conflict gets worse**: Texting can quickly escalate conflicts. The lack of immediate feedback can lead to a back-and-forth exchange that intensifies emotions and deepens misunderstandings.
5. **Permanent Record**: Text messages create a permanent record of what was said in the heat of the moment. These records can be revisited, prolonging the conflict and resentment. Recently I had a client in this situation. During our session, she deleted the texts so that she would not keep going back to them.
6. **Impersonal Nature**: Texting is more impersonal than a face-to-face conversation or a phone call. I know I have been guilty of hiding behind a text versus picking up a phone and calling the person.
7. **Delayed Responses**: Waiting for a response can prolong negative feelings and cause further stress. Have you ever thought because someone wasn't responding right away that they were mad? Sad? Angry? Or you conjure up a whole bunch of reasons for what they are thinking, but you seriously have no idea. Then you find out that maybe they did respond and forgot to hit send. I know I have done this.

ALTERNATIVES TO TEXTING WHEN UPSET

- **Face-to-Face Conversations**: If possible, discuss the issue in person. This allows for a richer and deeper connection.

- **Phone Calls**: If meeting in person is not an option, a phone call can help you explain yourself better.
- **Wait and Reflect**: Give yourself time to cool down and reflect on the situation before responding. This can help you approach the conversation more calmly and assume positive intent.
- **Writing a Draft**: If you must write, consider drafting your message and reviewing it later. Think before you talk.

These are some ways I have learned to navigate communication in its many forms.

Another way to navigate communication is in the art of listening.

The art of listening is a very important skill to learn that will help in building meaningful relationships, understanding others, and creating deeper connections. It goes beyond simply hearing words; it involves being fully present, listening with a caring ear, and being engaged with the speaker.

One of the ways to listen is to learn how to truly pay attention to whomever you are listening to. How many times have you been listening to someone and really what you are doing is contemplating your response to whatever they are saying?

Are we listening just to give our feedback, our perspective, or are we listening so we can learn their perspective, their feelings, and their emotions?

What I have noticed is when we listen with the other person in mind, versus ourselves, we create a connection with the other person. This doesn't mean we will always agree with the other person, but we will make them feel seen, heard, and valued.

Being a great listener encourages the speaker to go deeper by asking open-ended questions that invite more thought and elaboration. Questions like "How did that make you feel?" or "What do you think about that?" show curiosity and genuine interest.

I love thinking of this even from a spiritual perspective. Jesus was always asking questions. Why do you think this is? I believe it was to help people see themselves. Introspection.

This reminds me of the familiar story in John 8 of the woman taken in adultery. In this passage Jesus is confronted by religious leaders who bring a woman to him to be stoned. Jesus just writes in the sand. They keep asking him what he is going to do about this woman. So he says, "All right, but let the one who has never sinned throw the first stone". And this is the part I just love - when the accusers heard this, they slipped away one by one, beginning with the oldest, until only Jesus was left in the middle of the crowd with the woman.

They saw themselves. None of us are perfect. We all make mistakes.

Have you ever found yourself forming an opinion on a topic before you even finished listening to what someone was sharing?

I know I am guilty. Are you willing to "see yourself"?

Have you ever had a child come home from school, seemingly irritated, or a spouse coming home from work, and they are trying to share with you, and you are half-heartedly listening?

I am pretty sure we all have.

How different would it be if we stopped to truly listen and we could even say, "It sounds like you're feeling frustrated because of what happened at work/school. Is that right?"

We don't even need to fix anything. Maybe all they need is a listening ear. A caring heart.

Since we are talking about the "power of words" in this chapter, it is good to consider that in the power, is also the power of being silent in our listening.

Not thinking we have to say something all the time.

I love seeing relationships mend, marriages become more meaningful, families reconnect, all because of being willing to pay attention to how we communicate, what we say, what we don't say, and of course, being willing to say, "I messed up. I failed. I was wrong."

As I am writing this part of the book around the power of the words we speak, something came up for me that seriously is bringing tears to my eyes as I type. (If I was writing on paper versus typing, you would probably see tears stains on the paper.)

I had a memory that often would come up for me. I kept it to myself for probably 40-plus years, and just in the last few, I have thought of it often. I felt horrible about it. I knew I wanted to tell this person that I am sorry. She might not even remember, but that is beside the point. If it's bothering me, I want to fix it. I need to fix it.

I was with this person over a year ago, when this memory popped up again, while writing. She just happens to be my bestie of life. Her name is Barbie. Well really, it's Barbara but I have only ever called her Barbie, so it sticks. We have been friends for 46 years as of this writing. She truly is one of my favorite humans. We met on the monkey bars at Arnold Elementary School when we were 10 years old. Another friend of mine had just moved out of state and I was sad. I had stayed home from school for two days because I couldn't imagine going to school without my friend who had moved.

My mom said it was time to get back to school. That day I went to school and during recess I saw Barbie on the monkey bars. I don't remember what we talked about that day, yet I do know that ever since she has been my best friend. I even adore her entire family. The memories of growing up together are such a great part of my life. I always loved going to her parent's home after school and seeing her mom who was always there. Her mom always had cake. Oh, my goodness, I love cake. Her mom would listen to our struggles in school and just love us.

We were bridesmaids in each other's weddings, we raised our kids to know each other, they attended our kids' weddings and even came to Thailand with us for one of our son's weddings.

We've helped each other through some difficult times. Although we don't see each other as often as I'd like because of distance, it's one of those friendships where every time we are together, we pick up right where we left off.

In the last couple of years, every so often, I find myself remembering something I told her that I feel really bad about.

She grew up in a loving Christian home too, with wonderful parents teaching her about God and Jesus. One day as we walked home from school I said, "If you don't go to my church you will go to hell." I can't believe I said that. Yet in my young little mind of probably 12 years old, for some reason, I believed that to be true.

My heart truly hurts when I remember having said that.

Thankfully, when I asked her recently to forgive me, she said she doesn't remember it as such. Thank God. She does remember us talking spiritually around that time, as we often did, and still do, yet instead she said it was more from a place of fascination as to why our church had so many rules. Trust me, I wondered about that, too. She knew we both believed in Jesus. And she knew that church was not a building but rather our hearts. And I am grateful today that we both know that serving God isn't about rules, it's about a relationship with Jesus. That is so freeing.

Everyone needs a Barbie. A friend who loves you unconditionally.

So, whether it's words someone says to us, or words we say to others, we must consider the power they can hold. For the other person, and also for ourselves.

I am so glad I asked her to forgive me, even if her recollection of the talk wasn't what I had exactly remembered it to be.

Because it brought peace to my heart.

I love these quotes:

"Be careful with your words. Once they are said, they can only be forgiven, not forgotten." -Unknown

"Don't mix bad words with your bad mood. You'll have many opportunities to change a mood, but you'll never get the opportunity to replace the words you spoke." -Unknown

Favorite scriptures regarding what we speak:
It's not what goes into your mouth that defiles you; you are defiled by the words that come out of your mouth.
(Matt. 15:11 NLT)

If you want to enjoy life and see many happy days, keep your tongue from speaking evil and your lips from telling lies.
(1 Pet. 3:10 NLT)

When you take control of your words, you take back your life!

Remember, this very day, as you read this chapter of the book, you will have many opportunities to use your words. In your interactions with the people who cross your path — family, friends, co-workers or complete strangers — you can utter words that instill hope, wholeness and courage to others. Or your statements can kill — dashing dreams, crushing confidence and dragging someone's spirit down.

Whether you are speaking face-to-face, talking on the phone

or even using digital tongues in a comment thread or text message, remember there is power in your words.

HERE ARE three journal prompts to help you reflect on the power of your words:

1. **Reflect on Your Inner Dialogue:** Think about the words you speak to yourself throughout the day—even the ones you don't say out loud. What common phrases or thoughts have you noticed? How do these words make you feel, and how might your day change if you replaced any negative self-talk with kind, encouraging affirmations?
2. **Remember the Impact of Words:** Recall a time when someone's words, whether kind or hurtful, stayed with you for a long time. Write about that moment. How did those words shape your feelings or behavior afterward? What did you learn about the lasting power of language from that experience?
3. **Mindful Communication in Relationships:** Think about a recent conversation with a friend, family member, or colleague. How did your chosen words effect the interaction? Were there moments when you wished you'd spoken differently? Reflect on one specific instance and consider how you might use your words to build up and heal in future conversations.

These prompts are meant to help you explore how the words you use—and the words you hear—can either uplift or wound, shaping both your inner world and your relationships. Enjoy your reflection time!

CHAPTER 8
TRUST OVER CONTROL: THE SHIFT THAT TRANSFORMED MY LIFE

"Trust in the LORD with all your heart, and do not lean on your own understanding." (Prov. 3:5-6 NLT)

"Dear brothers and sisters, when troubles of any kind come your way, consider it an opportunity for great joy. For you know that when your faith is tested, your endurance has a chance to grow. So let it grow, for when your endurance is fully developed, you will be perfect and complete, needing nothing." (James 1: 2-4 NLT)

A saying that you will hear me often say is, "Trust and Control cannot coexist."

I honestly don't remember where I first heard that, and yet, it's been key to my life.

Let me tell you about an experience that really changed my life and helped me to have less stress and anxiety in my heart.

My daughter was 18 at the time and she was dating a guy who was not good for her.

(I have asked permission to tell this story.)

He seemed to be ok at first. I knew he had some of his own struggles from living with a controlling father. This kid was a star athlete. I witnessed several times when this kid would miss winning a race or something by an inch or so, and the dad would just give it to him, yelling at him from the stands. It broke my heart to watch this.

I left a few track meets cringing as I knew he would be yelled at more by his father.

I tried helping him. He honestly was worried he would become like his dad.

I tried to assure him that he didn't need to be. We all can make choices for our own lives that are different than the person who has negatively impacted it.

He tried.

And then he started making really bad choices, doing drugs, and hanging out with the wrong crowd.

And my daughter was dating him.

Of course, as a mother, I was a mess, to say the least.

I was always on her about this guy, secretly wishing she would ditch him.

I would often say, "Why are you with him? Why are you going out again?" I was that mother and I am sure I was driving her crazy.

But she was my daughter, I love her, and like most moms, we want what is best for our kids, right?

He broke up with her many times and they'd get back together again. I lost count of how many times that happened.

I was sick about it. I could see the controlling nature of him, and I sure didn't want my daughter dating or ultimately marrying someone like that.

My husband, the patient father that he is, would tell me that it would all work out. To let her be. Oh, my goodness, that was hard.

One night she left our house, late, to head over to his place again.

I sat on the couch, alone. The house was basically dark, except for a small light on. My husband had gone to bed. And I cried. I prayed, and I begged God to help me. To help her.

What was I to do? How do you help a young girl, your daughter, realize that she has more value than what this dude is showing to her?

And then, the most amazing experience happened.

I truly felt like Jesus was sitting right next to me. It was so comforting.

And I felt this question come to me, "Darla, when are you going to give your daughter to me?"

And I remember saying, "Now Lord, she's yours." I was so desperate.

I don't know if anyone who has kids and is reading this book can relate to this.

We want what's best for our kids, and yet we try to control the situation. I sure was.

And I was reminded again that trust and control cannot coexist.

We say we trust God, and then we are constantly being that parent that is frustrated, upset, crying, asking our teens why they are making stupid choices, dating the idiot, all the things, right? Surely, I am not the only one.

That night I went to bed and every time I awoke, wondering if she was home, if she was safe, I would pray, "She's yours Lord".

The next day she called telling me that she and this guy were headed to San Francisco to visit his friends (which I knew were not a good influence). And it was pouring rain.

I also knew that neither he, nor our daughter, were working at the time, so any gas in the tank was probably some that I had bought. And I knew that I owned the car and paid the insurance.

They happened to call when I was in my car driving with a friend. When my daughter told me where they were going, I answered, "Ok, I love you, be safe," and hung up.

My girlfriend looked at me, and I could tell on her face that she was shocked at how I had responded.

She said, "Are you ok with that?"

To which I replied, "NO! Not at all. But this morning, I gave her to God. I said, 'She is Yours.' And if I try to take her back, I get this vision of myself pulling her back in, as if I'm slapping Jesus in the face and saying, 'Just kidding, I don't believe You.'"

Now I don't know about you, but I don't ever want to let Jesus think that I don't believe in Him. I love Jesus so much.

For months after that, every single day, in my prayers, I would pray for her and I'd simply say, "She is yours".

No stipulation, no buts, just, "She is yours."

Now, don't think this was easy for me, it was very hard. I wanted to control this situation. I wanted this chapter of her life to be over, and yet I had to learn to be patient and wait.

As I have looked back at the experience many times, I now know that this experience was just as much for me as it was for her. God was seeing how much I was going to trust.

And not control.

Let me tell you the rest of the story...

I continued that simple, powerful, prayer. I was amazed at how often I would awaken in the night, and say, "She's yours.".

Seriously, I think God speaks to me most at night. Keeps me wide awake, wishing for sleep and when I finally stop fighting and I surrender my worries to Him I can go to sleep.

One night about two to three weeks later, my daughter came

home and asked if I had noticed she hadn't been going out with him anymore.

(Obviously, if your kids are in danger or in trouble with the law, you have to intervene. You can still pray so that you will have guidance on what to do, where to go and how to help.)

I had wondered, and yet I was not questioning. I had to trust. Ugh, it was hard, and yet so worth it.

She had noticed that I had changed too. I wasn't the nagging, frustrated mom I had been. I wasn't asking her all the questions of why she was going out with him, when she would be back, why she was wearing what she was…

Oh, my goodness, this was sooooo hard for me.

Seeing the changes that continued on in her life have been nothing short of amazing. Answered prayers. She has taught me so much and I love the relationship that we have today.

There will be times you trust and times you just don't. We are human and I am so grateful God knows this. God knows your hurt. He cares.

There are going to be times in your life too that you will be disappointed, even in others.

Experiences are going to come your way that really shake you, make you question your place, where you belong. You might even experience anger, frustration, and doubt. You might even question God.

You will wonder which direction you should go. One day you will feel like you know the answers and the next day, or even minute, you will question what is up. You might even fall to your knees in prayer and beg God for help. I actually hope you do. It helps.

There will be times in your life, whether in relationships or in business, at church even, that you will feel torn, confused, and forsaken. Lost.

Some of you right now, even as you read this, are experiencing some really hard stuff. Life is not what you had imagined it would be for yourself or your family.

Whether it's helping your kids navigate health challenges or watching them grow up and make decisions you don't agree with. I really feel for parents I know that have had to work through the really hard stuff of maybe a child doing drugs and partying all the time. Making decisions you just are sick about.

I've had friends whose children ran away, missing for days.

Or their children overdosed and died. The hurt and the triggers their families experience are unimaginable. I know my heart hurts for them so much.

And those are days I want you to remember to trust. To pray. Believing.

You will want answers today. "Like now would be good, God." You will get really tired of waiting. You will want the outcome to be what you think it should be.

I was talking to someone recently who is going through something really hard and we both were mentioning how we often want to say to God, "Yesterday would be nice Lord!"

Like could you get on it now? And our patience is truly tested.

Even as I write this book, I am realizing that God is trying to teach me patience in the current life experiences.

There have been times in the last year as we have worked through all that was happening in the church, in our lives, that I was so desperate. I look back now, thankful for those times.

Thankful? Yes, because God has been teaching me so much about myself. About His Will. About his timing.

He's had to show me some really ugly parts of my heart that needed to be looked at. He was and is teaching me to love others who sometimes, quite honestly, are not always easy to love.

One moment I will never forget is being so sad about all that was happening, how could this be and I just fell to the ground in my living room and sobbed in prayer. I was so desperate for answers, for direction. God saw and felt my need. And He provided. He still is providing.

We say we trust, but do we?

We want the perfect job now. We want all our relationships to be perfect now. We can't figure out why our business isn't where we want it to be, now. We don't understand why God hasn't brought us the right person yet, or why we are waiting so long to have a baby, or another baby…

So many things we just want NOW.

Get where I am going with this? And yet, life doesn't work that way.

It's like I shared before, with the BE, DO, HAVE concept. We think we need to have it all before we know joy, before we know peace. But the peace comes from trusting.

This makes me think of Simon in scripture when God was basically telling him to try one more time. He had fished all night and hadn't caught anything and scripture says this,

"Master, we worked hard all night and caught nothing…" (Luke 5:5 NIV)

Can you just picture this? I am sure Simon Peter was frustrated, tired, and maybe even hungry. I can almost hear him saying, "Do I really have to do this again?"

We often want a loud response, almost like an answer posted on a big billboard, telling us what way to go, what to say to someone, and how to forgive even.

Simon decided, "…Because You say so, I will let down the nets." (Luke 5:5 NIV)

And I love the result.

"When they had done so, they caught such a large number of fish that their nets began to break." (Luke 5:6 NIV)

Isn't that incredible? It kind of felt like Simon Peter was doubting what the result would be, and yet he moved forward and trusted, in spite of his doubts.

Many of us want to trust God. When times are good, it can feel easier. But when times feel difficult, it is even more important to trust God. God's unchanging character can give us a firm foundation when things feel unsteady and uncertain.

Often life goes along smoothly for quite a while. Your job is going well. Your friends and family are enjoyable and everyone is getting along. Your goals, finances, health and attitude toward life seem bright. Then, all of a sudden, life throws a curveball. Someone you know gets sick. Your bestie or family member gets a cancer diagnosis. You lose your job. A friend or family member betrays you. Maybe you find out that people you trusted in your entire life aren't who you thought they were. The things you felt secure in all of a sudden feel shaky and uncertain.

Life happens.

How do you trust that God is good in these circumstances? How do you trust Him when you do not understand what is happening? How do you trust Him when your health is failing, and tests are coming back with results you would rather not have? These are valid questions, and God wants to help you through these times.

Makes me think of a verse in scripture that says, "For I can do everything through Christ, who gives me strength." (Phil. 4:13 NLT)

I find myself writing that verse down many times a week in my journal to remind myself. I find myself reciting this often throughout the day.

It's crazy how I can know this, I can believe it, and yet I have to remind myself over and over.

WHAT DOES it mean to even trust? The definition I found is: *To trust is to believe in the reliability, truth, ability or strength of something.*

Trusting God is more than a feeling; it's a choice to have faith in what He says even when your feelings or circumstances would have you believe something different.

It doesn't mean we disregard our feelings or the reality of life. It's not pretending everything is OK when it is not and it's not living like an ostrich with our heads in the sand.

Trusting God for myself means trusting and believing in God even when life is difficult and I don't understand.

I have thought so much lately about patience and how this connects with trusting God.

I can bet you are similar to me in this.

We have goals, ideas of what we think life should look like, be like.

Even for my business right now as I type this, incredible opportunities are opening up. Opportunities for future speaking engagements, I am creating new programs, being asked to write for magazines, quite a few things, and yet I want it all done, right now.

And yet at the same time as opportunities are opening up, my humanness gets discouraged as to why my client schedule fluctuates so much.

I want to see that this book is received well, I want to see where God leads me spiritually, who he connects me with. Even whether I will have enough money to retire. Can I help my husband retire sooner? You know, all the things we think about.

I must be patient, keep doing what is put on my heart to do and keep moving forward.

I don't believe that God expects me to know the how in all he has asked us to do. He just wants to know my belief in Him.

I must trust and not control.

I love that He has proven over and over to me that when I do trust, and stop trying to control the outcome, the results are amazing. Blessings come. Miracles happen.

I bet you are asking, "Ok, fine, I get this whole trust thing but now what?? How do I even do this?"

I want you to think for a moment about someone you really trust. I bet you can tell them anything, right? You can be vulnerable, you can be upset, angry, cry, laugh, all the emotions and they still love you and they still listen and care, right?

Guess what? God is even more reliable than your best friend.

Makes me think of some favorite verses of mine.

"Cast all your anxiety on Him because He careth for you!" Pet. 5:7 NIV)

Or this one

"Come to me, all you who are weary and burdened, and I will give you rest." (Matt. 11:28 NIV)

I REMEMBER years ago going through some hard stuff. I was wide awake worrying about a relationship I had and it was hurting my heart.

I told you, God is always speaking to me during the night.

I remember the next day going on a long walk by myself and I just recited that verse and I would repeat it as though Jesus was talking to me right then, "Darla, just come, just come".

What I think is so amazing about that experience is that here I am years later, and I remember what I did. I remember giving it to God, yet I have no idea in my memory of what even was bothering me at that time. God took it from me, so I didn't need to worry about it anymore…oh how I love that.

Just realizing that again brings tears to my eyes of the gratitude I feel in my heart for prayer.

I want to learn to trust more and do this all the time. I am not perfect at this and never will be. Yet I am so grateful I have seen what happens when I do, and it makes me trust all the more.

Have you been trying to control the uncontrollable? But what if, instead, you focus on your response to whatever is thrown at you? You will be glad you did, and amazed at how life changes for you.

Trust and control cannot coexist.

HERE ARE three journal prompts to help you reflect on the themes of trust versus control in this chapter:

1. **Reflect on Letting Go:** Think of a time when you tried to control a situation because you feared the outcome. What was that experience like? Now, imagine how the situation might have changed if you trusted instead of controlling. Write about the feelings that arise when you consider letting go and allowing God or the process to guide you.
2. **Trust in Action:** Reflect on the moment when you decided to say, "She is Yours, Lord." What emotions were you experiencing in that moment of surrender? How did that decision impact your stress and anxiety? Describe what trust looks like for you and how it has transformed your approach to challenging situations.

3. **From Control to Peace:** Consider areas in your life where you currently feel the need to control outcomes—whether in relationships, work, or personal goals. Write about what it might feel like to shift your focus from controlling to trusting. What steps can you take to remind yourself daily that trust and control cannot coexist? How might this shift bring more peace and clarity into your life?

These prompts are designed to guide you in exploring how releasing control can open the door to deeper trust, transformation, and ultimately, a more peaceful heart.

CHAPTER 9
WHAT'S IN YOUR BACKPACK? UNPACKING EMOTIONAL WEIGHT

"Therefore, since we are surrounded by such a huge crowd of witnesses to the life of faith, let us strip off every weight that slows us down, especially the sin that so easily trips us up. And let us run with endurance the race God has set before us." (Heb. 12:1 NLT)

What type of "weight" are you carrying around?

After years of coaching my clients, it's been so apparent to me that the reason so many clients come for coaching truly is not the real reason.

There is almost always an underlying reason.

Let me give you an example from a client who hired me years ago to coach him.

"Don" had been referred to me by someone we knew.

He came to me to help him lose 40 pounds. I will never forget that discovery call. He was frustrated with life, trying to lose weight, and not understanding why he was having such a difficult time doing so.

Within a session or two, I knew that the weight he was holding on to was not just the physical weight, but it was much deeper than that.

He proceeded to share and uncover some real-life struggles and trauma he had experienced in his life.

My client, in a matter of a few months, lost his daughter and his marriage was on the rocks. They ended up divorced.

So here we were, years later after this difficult, horrible experience.

One day during our session, we were on video, I asked him to talk to me as though I was his spouse. To talk to the spouse (me) and tell me everything he wished she had said, that never had before.

Oh, if you could have seen this experience. Tears were flowing. He had no forewarning I was going to even ask this, so everything he was saying was not thought out beforehand but was flowing from his heart space.

He amazed himself that day to see all that was held up inside of him, stuck, and heavy like a brick.

He left that session with the homework to journal this experience as well.

Then in our next session, as I watched on video, he turned around and shredded his journal pages in the shredder. I could see the emotions of the experience. Tears and yet even relief.

He was releasing the trauma.

This is not easy by any means.

So many times, we are holding on to prior afflictions, past relationships, and the guilt of denying ourselves what we really needed out of life.

Many people hold on to some really difficult stuff, and it keeps them hostage or a prisoner in their own cages.

You can't just simply let go and will yourself to not care anymore. Many people, sometimes even your family and friends, expect you to just let go and yet it requires a process. It takes time.

I was so impressed with this man. I mostly have coached women and yet seeing Don so willing to do the work, to let go, to release his trauma, so he could become the healthiest version of himself was so incredible.

Little by little, release happens.

Our sessions together eventually ended. It was time for him to move forward and use the tools he had learned.

Seeing the change in his heart and life was amazing.

We hadn't spent much time talking about the 40 pounds on the scale, but rather on the weight he had been carrying.

When he was willing to let go of the mental weight, it helped the rest of his life to change.

About a year later, I got a message that made me so grateful.

He had attended a family wedding where it was planned that he would sit at the table during the reception with his son next to him and the ex-wife on the other side of the son. He messaged me after the wedding to let me know that for the first time in years, he was able to be in the same room, at the same table as the ex, and not feel anger.

He had begun to learn how to release the emotion of the trauma he had experienced.

And he lost 40 pounds.

The super cool part is just recently I was invited to his wedding. I had never met him in person, only on Zoom. However, I felt like I knew him from all our sessions together and his willingness to be vulnerable and let go of what was keeping him stuck.

His fiancee had attended a women's event I had hosted the

year prior so I got to meet her, but attending the wedding was the first time I would get to see him.

At the wedding, when everyone else stood to watch his bride come down the aisle, I instead looked at him up at the front with his groomsmen. I felt a tear come as I thought of this man, so willing to do the inner work to get to this point in his life.

It was wonderful.

We often carry weight on our shoulders. Healing comes when we are truly ready to let go of what is really causing the weight.

How often have you felt you were carrying some weight that was/is holding you down? That overbearing and all-consuming heaviness that presses down on you.

Each moment in our lives is defined by the emotion we feel that accompany it; how it affects us and what it evokes within us.

The weight we carry is the weight of so many things: responsibility, obligation, necessity, relationships, judgment.

Yet this weight can be so harmful to us. Stress-riddled lives need a way to cope, and what we often turn to is not always positive and can cause more harm to our lives. We carry this weight, hoping that it will make us stronger, hoping beyond all hope, that one day we'll have the life we want.

When people don't deal with the burdens, the weights, and the bricks in their backpacks, what happens is people often turn to unhealthy behaviors or addictions.

Imagine a backpack that we continually keep loading up. We keep stuffing it full of more and more bricks so that pretty soon we can't even zip the backpack up. Then the stuff starts spilling out all over the place, making a mess.

Plus, the backpack is so darn heavy.

That's what people often do in their lives.

It hurts my heart because I have seen so many people in my life who may struggle with alcohol addictions, drugs, and even sex addictions. I just care so much for their hearts because there is a story underneath all that.

I have really been noticing people as I am out and about in life. The homeless man lying in the park, asleep, surrounded by a pile of his belongings. I care about his story.

Or maybe it's the woman who happened to be out walking down the Main Street in our town. I was out too, just enjoying my morning walk and I noticed her, or should I say, heard her yelling obscenities over and over, to no one in particular. She was obviously high on something.

It didn't make me mad. It caused me to feel sad for her. What's her story? What led her to get to that point in her life?

Or what about your friend, she appears like she has it all together, and yet underneath all her makeup, perfect house, and seemingly perfect life, she is miserable. Maybe her husband is cheating on her. Maybe she is still carrying some trauma from her past that no one knows about. Or she wishes for a better relationship with her parents but can't get herself to forgive for how she was raised.

The people we would least suspect are hurting, are hurting.

What about the local business owner? She seems successful, looks like her life is all together, and yet she's hurting. A lot. She's married to someone who is narcissistic. She's lost all confidence in herself because she's been talked down to for years.

Her backpack is full. And she's not sure how to remove a brick. Or two.

And if she keeps going on, not addressing what is truly happening, her backpack just becomes heavier and heavier.

And yet there is hope. There is healing.

People can move on, let go of burdens, and let go of their trauma when a decision is made to start building something new.

To build a new life free from their past, free from whatever they have held on to, to create instead a new, although it might happen slowly.

Most of the time these are experiences, the trauma that people have held onto for years, so I love when they can show themselves grace as it gradually releases from their grasp.

But Darla, how do I do this?

First, they must first learn to love themselves enough, to want change.

As a Coach, I can't help anyone who isn't ready to be helped. Once someone decides they truly want change, even energetically things will begin to change.

Let me tell you about another client. Let's call her Cathy.

This lady is amazing. She owns several businesses, is single, and is creating a life for herself that is so different now than where she was before. She's a mom of two and a grandma.

Years ago, she came to me having left a marriage of over 35 years to a narcissist.

Her husband was very handsome and could say all the right things. I will never forget her sharing that sometimes he would tell her how beautiful she was and then the next day say that she repulsed him.

He controlled their household, their money, what they did, where they went, all the things. And he often drank way too much. Most people never knew. He could cover it up well. Others just saw him on the outside, the person he was in public.

She was miserable all the while trying to be the best mom she knew how to be to their two children.

And then he cheated on her and told her to leave and to get her own moving van.

Oh, my goodness.

These kinds of stories of clients sadly happen often. Women, and sometimes men, who are devalued, controlled, manipulated by their significant other.

I kept in touch with her for years before we worked together. Loving her right where she was at. And one day, she was ready. For true change, lasting change.

She was ready to be vulnerable. To stop hiding behind the facade of what was. In her words, "the big effect was me letting go of outdated dreams that were only holding me back from a better present and future."

She knew that in order to experience a better life she had to make changes. She had to be willing to do the hard.

Our sessions together were vulnerable. There were often tears, and over time I could start to see her release the stronghold he had on her and become stronger as a woman. If you could see her now - I am so proud of the inner work she has been willing to do.

Some people see vulnerability as a weakness due to cultural conditioning and ingrained social expectations.

Interestingly enough, vulnerability is one of the greatest strengths a person can have. It fosters genuine relationships, deeper connections, and personal growth. When people embrace it, they often find freedom, healing, and strength beyond what they imagined.

Are you holding on to bricks?

Are you in a relationship that makes you feel like you can barely breathe?

Are you ready to take some bricks out of your backpack?

Here are some ways to do that:

Removing bricks from your backpack involves identifying and addressing burdens or stressors in your life. Here's a few steps that could help you make that backpack a little lighter.

· · ·

1. **Identify Your Bricks**

   - **Reflect on Stressors:** Take some time to reflect on what feels heavy in your life. These could be emotional issues, work-related stress, relationship problems, health concerns, or anything else that feels like a burden. Often what we think is the stressor, really isn't. It's something deeper.
   - **List Them Out:** Write down each burden you identify. Sometimes, just acknowledging them can provide some relief.

2. **Prioritize and Assess**

   - **Rate Each Burden:** Assess the impact of each burden on your life. You can rate them on a scale of one to 10, with 10 being the most burdensome.
   - **Determine Control:** Identify which of these burdens you have control over and which you don't. Focus your energy on the ones you can influence. So much in our lives we try to control and realize that if we just let it go, because we truly can't control it, then friend, you will know more peace. (Remember the whole trust and control cannot coexist I talked about earlier?)

3. **Develop a Plan**

   - **Set Goals:** For each burden you can control, set specific, achievable goals. For example, if work stress is a burden, a goal might be to delegate tasks or speak with your manager about workload. I know someone who was very stressed out and even thought he was

having a heart attack. But by delegating some of his work responsibilities, he has felt better.
- **Break Down Actions:** Break down each goal into smaller, manageable steps. This makes the process less overwhelming.

4. Seek Support

- **Talk to Someone:** Sometimes discussing your burdens with a friend, family member, or therapist or even a life coach, can provide new insights and relief. I am often told from clients that just being able to have someone listen makes all the difference in their healing.
- **Professional Help:** Don't hesitate to seek professional help if needed. Therapists, counselors, and coaches can provide valuable support and strategies.

5. Practice Self-Care

- **Physical Activity:** Exercise can significantly reduce stress and improve your mood. For myself, I know exercise is key to my mental state. Walking is so helpful to me.
- **Mindfulness and Relaxation:** Practices like meditation, yoga, and deep breathing can help manage stress.
- **Healthy Lifestyle:** Ensure you're getting enough sleep, eating well, and taking breaks when needed.

6. Let Go of What You Can't Control

- **Acceptance:** Learn to accept the things you can't change. This might involve practicing mindfulness or

some breathing exercises to shift your mindset. (I have some breathing exercises you will find later in the book that really can help you.)
- **Focus on Positives:** Redirect your focus to the positive aspects of your life and things that bring you joy.

7. Regular Check-ins

- **Review Progress:** Regularly review your list of burdens. How are you doing?
- **Adjust as Needed:** Life changes, and so do your burdens. Adjust your strategies as necessary. What was maybe a brick before is maybe not even important to you anymore.

8. Set Boundaries

- **Learn to Say No:** Protect your time and energy by setting boundaries. Don't take on more than you can handle. Do you need to create a boundary around a certain person?
- **Create Balance:** Strive for a healthy balance between work, rest, and play.

PRACTICAL EXAMPLE

Let's say you've identified one of your bricks as a heavy workload. Here's how you might address it:

1. **Identify:** Realize that your workload is causing stress.
2. **Assess:** Rate it as a 9/10 in terms of burden.

3. **Plan:** Set a goal to reduce your workload by 20% over the next two months.
4. **Actions:** List steps like delegating tasks, prioritizing projects, and discussing with your manager.
5. **Seek Support:** Talk to a mentor or colleague for advice. Have you even shared with your management team how you are feeling? Maybe they have no idea how burdened you are feeling because you always seem to have it all under control.
6. **Self-Care:** Ensure you're taking breaks and not working overtime.
7. **Acceptance:** Understand that some busy periods are inevitable, but they are temporary.
8. **Check-ins:** Every week, review how your workload feels and adjust your strategies if needed.
9. **Boundaries:** Make it a rule to not check emails after a certain hour to ensure you have personal time. If you work at home like I do, I close my office door when I leave it, so I feel like I have gone home.

By addressing each brick one by one, you can lighten your load and boost your overall well-being.

HERE ARE **three journal prompts to help you explore the emotional weight you carry and begin the process of unpacking it:**

1. **Identify Your Bricks:** Take a few moments to list the "bricks" in your backpack. These could be past traumas, unresolved grief, guilt, or any burden you feel weighs you down. For each item, write a few sentences

about how it shows up in your daily life emotionally, mentally, and even physically. How does carrying this weight affect your relationships, decision-making, or sense of self?
2. **The Power of Letting Go:** Reflect on a time when you began to release some of this weight, perhaps when you finally acknowledged a difficult memory or chose to forgive. How did that experience change your outlook or your behavior? Write about the emotions you felt as you started letting go. What small steps did you take, and how did they create space for healing or new growth?
3. **Your Future, Lighter Self:** Imagine your life without these burdens. Write a letter from your future self who has learned to let go and live more freely. What advice or encouragement does this wiser version of you offer? How does the weightless version of yourself approach challenges, relationships, or new opportunities differently? What message do you need to hear today to help you start the process of unburdening?

These prompts are meant to help you acknowledge what you've been carrying, reflect on the impact it has had, and envision the freedom that comes from letting go. Enjoy the process of discovery and healing.

CHAPTER 10

FAITH BEYOND THE FAMILIAR: SEEKING TRUTH FOR YOURSELF

"See, I am doing a new thing! Now it springs up; do you not perceive it? I am making a way in the wilderness and streams in the wasteland." (Is. 43:19 NIV)

Have you ever heard of the pot roast story?

This young bride is making dinner for her new husband, and she decides she will make them a pot roast. So, she buys the pot roast and prepares it for the oven. Her husband happens to walk by the kitchen and notices that she's cutting the ends of the pot roast off before she puts it in the glass pan. He asks her why she's cutting the ends off, to which she replies, "I don't really know why I do that, except that's how my mother has always done it." Later as she's talking on the phone to her mom, she mentions that she made a pot roast. She decides to ask her mom, "Hey mom, why do you always cut the ends of the pot roast off before you put it in the glass pan?" The mom pauses, and says, "I don't know daughter, that's the way my mom always did it"'

The young bride is so puzzled by now that she decides to call her grandma and ask her the same question. To which the grandma replies, "I cut off the ends because I didn't have a big enough pan".

How many times have you done something, thought something, believed something, all because it's been done that way for as long as you can remember. And even the generations before you, that's all they knew.

No one thinks to ask, to wonder why, they just do it. Or they wonder, they even doubt and question to themselves, but they don't ask, they don't seek answers. Yet, all those years, meat was wasted that didn't need to be.

If they'd asked, or inquired, they would've been more knowledgeable, smarter even, and not continued to make a choice that makes no sense at all.

Or maybe they did ask, and were told, "That is just the way it is."

There are so many people walking blindly through life. They just keep doing what they have always done. I have done this too.

Think about the morning coffee ritual. Many of you prepare your coffee the same way every day because that's how you were taught. We might not even pause to consider if there's a more enjoyable or healthy way to start the day. Just as the bride followed a routine with the pot roast, we follow routines out of habit rather than intentional choice. I personally don't even drink coffee, but for years after I was married, I still bought Folgers coffee because that is what mom bought when I was a kid. I had no idea that many people don't even like that coffee now that all these fancier kinds have become available.

Think about something as simple as washing dishes. Maybe you're still using the same dish soap your parents always used, even though something different could work just as well or maybe even better. We tend to fall into that if it ain't broke, don't fix it mindset, don't we? But sometimes, holding onto old habits like this can keep us from discovering more efficient or even more meaningful options.

In the workplace, I see it all the time. We hold on to the same routines just because that's the way things have always been done. Maybe it's an old filing system or a meeting format that doesn't really work for anyone anymore. I've caught myself following these habits without ever stopping to ask, "Is there a better way?" And when I don't take that moment to reflect, I end up missing opportunities to improve or try something new.

My husband read a book a couple years ago called **"Managing Millennials For Dummies,** by Hannah L. Ubl (Author), Lisa X. Walden (Author), and Debra Albit (Author). As a Senior Project Manager for a commercial contracting company, he understood that his way, being older than the guys working for him, didn't mean that there couldn't be a better way to do some things than what he was currently doing. It also helped him to try and see how other generations look at life. Getting different perspectives is key to creating a better work environment.

Many family traditions are followed simply because they're familiar. For instance, you might celebrate holidays in a certain way and then life changes, your kids marry, the family grows, and you realize that change is good.

It's ok to not have turkey for Thanksgiving. (smile)

As our kids have grown up, married and began families of their own, we have had to see that change even around the holidays is good for us.

Our one daughter-in-law, Mari, and her family have the best Christmas Eve celebrations with all the relatives. They all get dressed up, have lots of gifts, stay up late, have dance parties, all the things. I think our Christmas celebrations are fun, but seriously, they aren't as fun as that!

When our son Kyle and Mari married, I couldn't imagine her not getting to experience that every year with her family, so we decided to create our own family tradition. We celebrate Christmas another weekend, usually over the New Year holiday time. It's actually worked out really well.

We all have those habits we follow without really questioning them - like the way that pot roast gets trimmed before it goes in the oven, simply because that's how it's always been done. And it got me thinking: if we can challenge everyday routines to find better, more meaningful ways of doing things, shouldn't we apply that same curiosity to our spiritual lives?

I'm so grateful I was raised knowing who Jesus is. I grew up watching my parents pray and read their Bibles, and I cherish that. But looking back, I wish I'd asked more questions as a kid or teen. I now see how important it is to really seek and learn for ourselves.

For most of my life, I stuck with the King James Version of the Bible, even though I often felt confused or lost in translation. I was told that the KJV was the only version I should read, but deep down, I felt like I was missing something. I started exploring other translations because I craved a clearer understanding, something that spoke truth about what was really important to God.

Years ago, I picked up the New Living Translation (NLT), and it was as if the Bible came alive for me. I'm not saying it's the only translation out there, as we know there are quite a few. But this translation helped to open my eyes, and to make me love reading my bible. I know I am not alone in this journey; many people have shared with me how they too, although reading the Bible regularly, never quite understood what they were reading and now are so enthralled with learning the scriptures more.

This all reminds me of Thomas from the Bible. Most people know him as doubting Thomas because he wasn't convinced about Jesus' resurrection until he saw proof. When his fellow disciples told him they'd seen the risen Christ, he insisted, "Unless I see the nail marks in His hands and put my finger where the nails were, and put my hand into His side, I will not believe" (John 20:25 NIV). But here's the thing: Thomas wasn't just being skeptical—he was earnestly seeking truth. And when Jesus appeared and invited him to touch His wounds, Thomas's response was immediate: "My Lord and my God!" (John 20:28). That moment wasn't about doubt; it was about a genuine, personal encounter with the truth of who Jesus is.

I love that about Thomas. His story is a beautiful reminder that God welcomes our questions. He wants us to seek, wrestle with, and ultimately discover truths that deepen our faith. I've learned that living for God isn't about following a set of man-made rules or traditions, rather it's about cultivating a personal relationship with Him. I've come to realize that for too long, I was more focused on the church as an institution than on Jesus Himself.

Our decisions are only as good as the information we have, and I had to plead with God to help me let go of any "truths" I clung to simply because that's how they were handed down. Now, I encourage you: ask God for guidance, seek out scripture, and be open to new revelations. Don't just take my word for it, discover your own truth through reading the bible.

Don't get stuck doing the same old thing, like chopping off the ends of a pot roast without ever knowing why. Ask questions. God invites you to ask, to seek, and to knock—and I promise, when you do, doors will open. (Luke 11:9, NLT)

. . .

Here are three journaling prompts to help you reflect on the ideas in this chapter:

1. **Questioning the Routine:** Think about a habit or tradition you follow simply because it's been done that way—like the pot roast story or even your morning coffee ritual. What's one area in your life where you feel stuck in a routine? How might asking why lead you to a new, more meaningful way of doing things? Is there a tradition that maybe if you switched it up a bit, there would be more harmony in the family?
2. **Seeking Spiritual Clarity:** Reflect on your journey with the Bible or your spiritual practices. Have you ever felt like you needed more clarity or a fresh perspective? What steps have you taken, or could you take, to discover a deeper, more personal understanding of God's truth?
3. **Embracing the 'Thomas' Within:** Consider a time when you questioned the way things were done and sought your own truth, much like Thomas did. How did that process of seeking change your understanding or faith? What questions are you still holding onto that might open up new paths in your spiritual journey?

These prompts are designed to help you explore where you might be holding onto old habits and how embracing a spirit of inquiry could lead to transformative insights in your life and faith.

CHAPTER 11
EVERY CHAPTER MATTERS: EMBRACING THE HARD TIMES THAT BUILD US

"Not only so, but we also glory in our sufferings, because we know that suffering produces perseverance; perseverance, character; and character, hope." (Rom. 5:3-5 NIV)

Now I believe wholeheartedly that every chapter matters. Every moment is important. Every chapter makes us who we are and yet some days I too, have felt that some chapters suck. Yep, I said it.

Dad, I am sorry. I know he hated that word suck.

Do you ever feel that way? I am pretty sure I just heard you say, "YES!" out loud while you are reading this.

Life is full of highs and lows, and it's natural for some chapters to be more challenging than others.

I don't think we would be completely honest if we said there wasn't a chapter in our life that was not difficult.

And yet I want you to look back over your life, at all the good times and even the bad.

Growth often comes with discomfort. During tough times, you might be learning new skills, adapting to new situations, or facing challenges that push you out of your comfort zone. This process, while painful, can potentially lead to living your best life. So be patient.

Sometimes, events happen that are beyond your control, such as the loss of a loved one, health issues, or economic downturns. These situations can be incredibly hard to get through. I already shared earlier about losing my dad, losing my brother, and going through the financial challenges. Those were not fun chapters in my life.

They sucked actually.

And yet I got through them.

And you can, too.

MAYBE FOR YOU or someone in your family, you have had to face some really difficult mental health issues such as depression, anxiety, or other disorders that can make even the most ordinary aspects of life feel unbearable. Seeking professional help in these cases can be crucial.

I love the words of a song by Katy Nichole, where she speaks of God being in the details, all the details.

What about comparison and expectations of others? We can easily get in a funk because we see others posting their amazing lives on Instagram and yet what you really don't know is they too are having a difficult chapter.

This whole comparison thing can be dangerous. We can easily focus on what we haven't done versus what we have. We see someone whose business is seemingly thriving, but we don't see the nights they lay awake worried, wondering how they would ever get ahead.

If you are having money problems, and it seems like there is always more month than money, this can add additional stresses to our lives and make a chapter in life seem really tough. I know that chapter for us was hard.

There have been many a month over the years when we took from one account to cover another one.

I am so grateful for those times now as it made me get serious about making changes that have led to where we are today.

When I think about some of what we have been through to get to today, I find myself laughing to myself. But for many years, it wasn't funny.

Life is like that, right? As we are in the midst of those challenging chapters, life is hard. Then years later we can look back and see that we needed to experience the hard stuff to make us the person we are today.

A book that really helped me on our financial journey is called, "MONEY, A love story." I highly recommend it. The author is Kate Northrup. She really helps you go back in your life and think about the money stories you have been telling yourself. I think I could write another book just on that subject.

I remember many conversations with our kids talking about chapters of life. When they were teenagers and in the midst of some hard stuff, it felt to them that they would never get out of the chapter they were in.

I assured them that if we try to remove a chapter, because we hate it, the next chapter will not make sense.

Take a moment, yourself, and think about this.

Everything you're going through right now, it will make sense one day.

It will. I promise.

Imagine your book is as old as you are right now as you read this.

Let's say you are on chapter 42 and you try to remove chapter 21, you know that year you were partying too much, staying out way too late, spending all your money, or even racking up the debt on those crazy credit cards.

And now as you write chapter 42, you are a different person, making better decisions, saving money, debt free, maybe you're married and a parent by now.

Can you look back and see why chapter 21 mattered? It helped shape who you are today.

For me, and my husband, we had some really hard chapters. The financial chapters of life, when we wondered if we'd ever get out of debt, have a savings account again, all the things, those were hard. Just because we can now travel more and do fun little get away trips with our family, doesn't mean it was always like that.

Now we are heading in a few years to the chapter where retirement starts for my husband and honestly, I find that a little scary. Will we have enough money to allow us to continue to live the life we have now?

Or those chapters when I lost my dad and my brother. Those were hard chapters too, and yet, here today, having had those experiences, I can now have more compassion and sympathy helping people as they maneuver those similar chapters in their lives.

I would never have known during those chapters that people would eventually hire me to coach them through their periods of grief.

And you know what? I've come to realize that even the chapters that really suck have a purpose. When you're in the middle of a tough phase, whether it's financial struggles, loss, or just those days when everything feels off, it's hard to see the light at the end of the tunnel. But those challenging pages for me, as painful as they were, taught me resilience, compassion, and grit.

I used to wish I could just erase the rough parts of my story, but now I see that every struggle added a new layer to who I am. Those moments of hardship weren't there to break me; they were there to build me up. I often jot down my thoughts in a journal, not to wallow in the pain, but to remind myself of the strength I discovered along the way. Every setback became a steppingstone, pushing me to grow and evolve, even when I couldn't see it happening in the moment.

So, as you flip through the chapters of your own life, remember that the bitter moments often make the sweet ones all the more meaningful. Every chapter, no matter how hard, has shaped you into the person you're becoming. Embrace them, learn from them, and know that even the roughest pages are an essential part of your unique story.

HERE ARE **three journaling prompts to help you reflect on the ideas in this chapter:**

1. **Reflect on Growth Through Challenge:** Think about a time in your life when you felt a chapter really sucked. What did you learn from that experience? How did it help build your perseverance or shape your character?
2. **Finding Meaning in the Tough Times:** In light of Romans 5:3-5, write about how a difficult season led you to discover hope or inner strength. What unexpected lessons emerged from that struggle?
3. **Embracing Every Chapter:** Consider your entire life story, the highs and the lows. How do even the hard moments contribute to the person you are today? What

might you say to your past self about the value of those challenging chapters?

These prompts are meant to help you see that every chapter, no matter how tough, plays a role in shaping your unique journey. Enjoy the reflection!

CHAPTER 12
WHEN "I'M FINE" ISN'T ENOUGH: THE HIDDEN COST OF PRETENDING

"The Lord is close to the brokenhearted and saves those who are crushed in spirit."(Ps. 34:18 NLT)

I was out walking by the canal the other day when I noticed the water, full to the brim, reflecting a flood of memories, memories I'd rather not think about. It wasn't really the canal that stirred these feelings; it was the way the sight of that overflowing water brought back a very difficult time in my life. Even writing about it now makes my heart race and anxiety creep in, yet I feel compelled to share in hopes that someone else might recognize their own hidden struggles.

At that moment, the song "Truth Be Told" by Matthew West was playing, and its lyrics hit me hard. When he talks about being fine but he's not, he's broken.

How many times have you said, "I'm fine" to friends or even to yourself, when deep down you're screaming, "I need help?" It's a phrase we use to mask pain, to pretend that everything is okay, even when we're far from it.

For me, that phrase takes me back to the days after our daughter was first born. She's 27 now. I remember sitting in the bathtub, overwhelmed by raging hormones and the uncertainty of postpartum depression. With a new baby to care for and two older boys who were thankfully old enough to dress themselves, I felt I should have it all together.

Yet, inside, I was terrified. I even imagined disappearing into the water, and I was overwhelmed by these thoughts. I prayed desperately for those dark thoughts to vanish, knowing I loved my family too much to let them see how broken I felt.

I tried to keep up appearances during the day, smiling, going through the motions, telling everyone, "I'm fine." But when night fell, the weight of it all returned: the fear of what I might do, the anxiety that crept in as I lay awake. I'd find myself reciting scripture—Philippians 4:8, urging myself to think on things that are pure and right—hoping to push the anxiety away.

Looking back, I realized how hard it was to admit I wasn't okay. I kept these feelings hidden, sharing them only with my husband, who held me through many tearful nights. I wish I'd sought help sooner.

If you're experiencing symptoms of postpartum depression or are struggling with overwhelming anxiety, whether after childbirth or during another challenging time, please know you are not alone. Reach out to a trusted friend, family member, or mental health professional. The American Psychological Association lists symptoms like persistent sadness, anxiety, irritability, changes in sleep or appetite, and even thoughts of self-harm. Recovery is possible, and you deserve support.

Eventually the tub experiences went away, thank God, and then they were replaced with these nighttime fears, almost like being afraid of the night.

This happened off and on for a few years, and usually during my cycle. I hated it.

I would delay going to bed because I was afraid I would have these thoughts again. And they only happened at night.

I could never pinpoint what was causing them, except to know it was cyclical and hormonal.

Seriously, hormones suck.

What has helped me through these experiences has been to make sure self-care is a priority, including exercise, eating healthy, and lots and lots of prayer.

I spent many a night begging God to remove these horrible thoughts, and he would help me so much.

Until they came back months, or years later. And I would do it all over again.

I know having my thyroid checked and knowing I have Hashimoto's, taking my low dose of Levothyroxine was also a big help.

I also personally love natural supplements, vitamins and patches that have helped my hormones and headaches.

I share my story not to dwell on the pain, but to remind you that it's okay to admit when you're not fine. Pretending everything is okay only deepens the hurt. Vulnerability isn't a weakness, it's a courageous step toward healing. When you stop saying "I'm fine" and start acknowledging your pain, you allow yourself the chance to receive the help and love you need.

I hope that by sharing my experience, you'll feel less alone and more empowered to be honest about your struggles. Let's choose truth over pretense and allow ourselves to be healed.

Remember, the Lord is near to the brokenhearted, and His strength is there to lift us when we feel crushed.

. . .

Here are three journaling prompts to help you reflect on the ideas in this chapter:

1. **The Mask of "I'm Fine":** Reflect on a time when you said "I'm fine" even though you felt something entirely different. What were you experiencing beneath that phrase? How did keeping your true feelings hidden impact you and your relationships?
2. **Honesty with Yourself:** Write about the barriers that make it hard for you to admit when you're not okay. What fears or beliefs prevent you from being vulnerable? How might acknowledging your true feelings lead to healing and greater peace?
3. **Seeking Support and Release:** Consider what support or actions you need when you're really struggling—beyond just saying "I'm fine." What steps can you take, or who can you reach out to, that would help you begin to unpack and release this hidden weight?

CHAPTER 13
"BEYOND MY UNDERSTANDING: DISCOVERING THE VASTNESS OF GOD"

"May the Lord answer you when you are in distress; may the name of the God of Jacob protect you." (Ps. 20:14)

Throughout this book, we've explored how our mindset, the words we speak, and our willingness to be vulnerable opens us up to God's transforming love. More than anything, my deepest hope is that you come to know that Jesus loves you just as you are. His love is immeasurable; it isn't confined to a building or a specific church. His love lives in the heart of every person.

This journey of honesty with myself connects to everything we've discussed so far about the power of our words, the strength of a transformed mindset, and the constant presence of God in our lives. When we stop trying to control our lives, and let go, we allow God's love to fill the empty spaces and transform our struggles into strength.

On a recent trip to Thailand in December 2023, my heart was still heavy with unanswered prayers and a longing for a miraculous sign. Both my husband and myself, without telling one another, had both been praying that while traveling we would see God at work in a new place.

One Sunday one of our sons wanted to take us to a lookout with an amazing view not too far from Chaing Mai. So off we went with our son, his wife Som and our grandson Bryce.

We drove a while until we came to a road barely wide enough for one car. It was a very windy and bumpy road.

We drove until we came upon a small village called Hang Dong-Ban Pong, where we encountered a gathering of local people. We asked our daughter-in-law, Som, to ask in her native language what the people were all gathered together for. It was Christians who had come together for their annual convention to give thanks for their blessings.

I wish you could've been there. There was a lady who spoke really good English who invited us to stay for the church service. Her name was Tik, pronounced Teek and she had the cutest son named Mitsu. She even told me she had named her son after their little SUV which was a Mitsubishi!

Although we couldn't understand the words being spoken, we felt the Spirit of God move powerfully among us. I remember leaning over to Som and asking her what the pastor was preaching on, and she said, "Moses." Tears streamed down my face as I realized that God had answered my prayer. And my husbands, too.

In that moment, I knew beyond any doubt that God was with me, guiding every step of my journey. He was answering prayers and giving me clarity.

He was going to help me make decisions for my life that I knew I could not make on my own.

God was helping me make decisions that I knew not everyone

would understand or agree with. And yet, I had to follow his guidance.

I knew this, I know this. I believe this. And it brings peace to my heart.

THERE WILL BE times when other people just don't understand our decisions. And will we be ok with that?

Do you think everyone understood David in 1 Sam 17?

David is this young shepherd boy who faced a giant warrior when no one else was willing. The Philistines and the Israelites were at war. Goliath, a nine-foot-tall Philistine, challenged the Israelites to send a man to fight him. David, who was just bringing food to his brothers in the army, volunteered to face Goliath with only a sling and five stones. With God's help, David killed Goliath with one stone and became a hero of Israel.

What if he never picked up the stone?

People thought he was crazy. How could this young lad possibly do this?

And yet, God provided.

After the church service was over, this same lady, Tik, insisted we all stay for their annual potluck of sorts. They all bring foods that they have grown or raised to share with one another. We were given so much food, some of which I had no idea what I was eating!

That day, that experience will forever be in my heart.

Remember, friend, His love is bigger than our doubts and more powerful than our fears.

He will answer our prayers in ways we never imagined.

The timing won't always be as fast as we'd like either.

His love is a love that invites us to trust Him fully, even when we don't understand the challenges before us.

As we move forward into the next section of this book (I'll share the healthy habits that have helped me navigate ups and downs to live a life where I have more energy, and feel better physically, as well as mentally.), I invite you to hold on to this truth: when we align our mindset with God's love and speak words that heal, we prepare ourselves not only for emotional healing but also for building a healthier, more vibrant life.

Remember: you are loved, you are not alone, and even in your moments of brokenness, God is with you.

ENCOUNTERING GOD'S VASTNESS: Journal Prompt

- Can you recall a moment when you felt overwhelmed or sensed a presence greater than yourself? Perhaps unexpectedly, like the experience of feeling God's love in a difficult situation. Describe that moment in detail. How did it shift your perspective on your struggles, and what message does it hold for you as you continue your journey toward healing and healthy habits?

CHAPTER 14
HEALTHY HABITS: SMALL STEPS TO A BETTER YOU

Don't you realize that your body is the temple of the Holy Spirit, who lives in you and was given to you by God? You do not belong to yourself, for God bought you with a high price. So you must honor God with your body. (1 Cor. 6:19-20 NLT)

"Good Habits are as Addictive as Bad Habits, And a lot more rewarding" -Harvey MacKay

Personally, I think the word habit can get a bad rap. Yes, there are bad habits that a person creates for themselves which can lead them down a path of destruction, and yet I am here to tell you that you can create healthy habits, happy ones, that when learned, will allow you to live a life of more satisfaction.

Healthy habits are the building blocks of our lives; small, consistent actions that create lasting change. As the habit changer, I've seen firsthand how actions like drinking more water, eating nourishing foods, moving our bodies, and journaling can have a profound impact on our well-being. In this section, we're going to explore how these simple habits can shape our lives in meaningful ways, helping us become the healthiest, most vibrant versions of ourselves. Together, we'll break it down step-by-step and start building a foundation that makes thriving physically, mentally, and spiritually a natural result.

I have been asked multiple times how I became a life coach and how I began focusing on the mindset of life and healthy habits, and I will tell you that it is because I had to learn them myself. I was struggling as you read in the first part of the book. Not only did I experience physical health issues, but I also was dealing with stress and some anxiety. I knew I had to change. I couldn't expect different results without making changes myself. I was responsible for my change, for my wellness.

So often our habits aren't serving us, and we aren't even aware of it.

That reminds me of when I was in high school. You will remember from earlier that I had grown up with headaches, stomachaches, and allergies, and no one had ever told my mom when I was a kid that it could possibly be from what I was eating.

In high school, it was quite common for my bestie Barbie (Her real name is Barbara but I still call her Barbie! The same Barbie I mentioned earlier!) and I to go to the vending machines during lunch and grab ourselves a Diet Coke and a Mother's brand of Chocolate, Chocolate Chip Cookies. I didn't think at all that this was possibly causing some of the health issues I was having. Now I know not everyone was/is affected by certain foods, but I sure was. I still am.

I bet more people are affected, that don't realize it or don't want to acknowledge it. But, instead continue to eat whatever they want and wonder why they have headaches, stomachaches, and indigestion.

Even now, the strangest things make me itch. Certain brands of tea, for instance. I love iced tea, and certain restaurants have a brand of iced tea that for whatever strange reason makes me get phlegm in my throat and I will start to itch on my feet, my head, my hands. That is one of the ways our body will "talk" to us that what we are eating is causing a sensitivity to our body.

Have you noticed that every time you eat a certain food, maybe its dairy, that you are running to the bathroom? Or you eat something spicy because you love it, but then you are doubled over in pain?

Friend, that is your body's way of saying, "Please don't eat that!"

How about someone who goes to Starbucks all the time, ordering those coffee drinks that are ladened with sweeteners. Then they are hungry so they grab a Danish or two, and they do this day after day, but don't stop to consider how this habit of all this sugar is affecting their health.

We often don't pay attention to how our bodies are feeling.

Doing this occasionally isn't going to kill you, and yet it's when we do it day in and day out that we need to be concerned.

I know I have been guilty of standing at the refrigerator and staring at it when I was not even hungry. Or reaching in the cupboard to grab something totally unhealthy that I will shove down my mouth while aimlessly watching a Netflix show.

Rest assured, it's not just you. I have done it, too.

And being that I am not perfect, sometimes I resort to making a choice to eat something that I know will cause me to not feel well.

I have found it is easier not to buy some foods that I just love, such as Barbecue potato chips. I could eat the entire bag. Goodness, I wish I had some right now while I am writing this.

It's crazy to think that we actually create what I refer to as a

Habit Loop. We get triggered by something, maybe a location that brings memories flooding back in, or a certain time of day triggers us, a social situation, or even a person.

Then what happens next is this trigger creates a behavior, a routine. Maybe for you, it's overeating or smoking, or maybe it's drinking way too much alcohol, or biting your nails so short that they bleed.

And then that behavior leads to a reward, which isn't always the best.

An example of this might be you are out shopping and from across the store you see your ex-boyfriend who was a total jerk to you. So, it triggers you and the next thing you know, you are eating everything in sight, or you grab a few too many beers and you find that you gained weight, or you went into complete stress mode.

That's an example of a habit loop that we want to break, my friend.

How do we break a habit loop?

Start by identifying what is causing the trigger to happen. Awareness is the beginning of change. Maybe for you it's a specific time of day, an emotional state, a certain place, or an interaction with a particular person.

Once you recognize what triggers you, try to change it. For example, if stress triggers your habit of snacking, find a healthier way to cope with stress, such as taking a walk or practicing deep breathing exercises.

Replace the routine associated with the habit with different, healthier behavior. If you tend to check your phone first thing in the morning, try replacing that routine with a few minutes of stretching or journaling.

Don't expect that you are going to do this overnight, my friend. This will take some time. Be patient with yourself.

Let's create new habits. Healthy ones.

Don't beat yourself up over the "negative" habit. Let's instead focus on the habit you want to create.

The definition of a habit is, "a settled or regular tendency or practice, especially one that is hard to give up."

So, if that is the definition of habit, why can't it be also a good habit?

Or as I will call them, a healthy habit.

The way to let go of the unhealthy habits of your past, whatever those are, is to rewrite the script, the narrative of what you have been giving them.

Positive and affirmative self-talk is powerful and yet I also know it can be hard to grasp or believe it will help you when you are experiencing anxiety or a panic attack and someone is telling you to just relax.

That can be annoying, right?

What I had to learn for myself to change my unhealthy habits, was to gradually start, one day at a time to do some healthier ones. Eventually I was feeling better, and I learned that I loved how I felt, mentally, physically, spiritually, depending on the habit, and I wanted to do them more.

You too, will begin to love how you feel from doing these healthy habits and it begins to make it easier to do them. You want the result, so you do the habit.

I have a client that is trying to implement movement into her day. A person can't go from not working out at all to thinking she is just going to go to the gym for an hour and a half a day and stay consistent.

Start slow. Maybe today you start by walking around the block, and then the next day you go a little bit farther.

Your habit could be learning to go to sleep at a similar time each night, so you are able to awake easier in the morning and stop hitting the snooze alarm one more time.

It's easy to get overwhelmed thinking of learning new habits and I am here to tell you it doesn't have to be.

What works for me is to show myself some grace on this journey. None of us will ever be perfect at this. And if we think we are, or will be, well, my friend, I have other news for you.

What helped me when I first started on my wellness journey was to focus on what I could have or do, not what I couldn't. No one wants to feel deprived.

If we talk just about changing our way of eating, we all know that there are a ridiculous number of diets and ways to lose weight. There are vegan, Mediterranean, paleo, ketogenic, intermittent fasting, low carb, Atkins, Weight Watchers and I am sure a bunch more.

I am sure you have heard of people going on these crazy diets, like only eating cabbage, or something crazy like that. Yes, they might lose weight temporarily, but I can almost guarantee you that they will gain it back.

And besides that, is that truly even living life? That is total deprivation. It is not sustainable. This was mind boggling: 40-80% gain back all the weight they have lost within five years.

The best way to maintain your weight loss is to continue to exercise, eat healthily, and avoid those unhealthy habits that you had let go of.

Often people want to lose weight, say 50 pounds, and they don't start because 50 pounds sounds overwhelming. Yet, I help them to see that we don't need to focus on the 50 pounds. Let's just focus on today, one day at a time. What can you do today? And then tomorrow, think about what you will do that day.

When thinking of beginning to change your previous habits,

the ones keeping you stuck to instead living healthy habits, a first step that is key is to love yourself.

Love yourself enough to make changes. You will thank yourself later, I promise.

It's ok if you fall off the wagon every once in a while. Just get back on.

Often our unhealthy behaviors are a sign of something much deeper. Most unhealthy habits are in reaction to stress: maybe you're working too much, or even hate your job, and you are staying because you need the money, or you've experienced loss, and worry, and you are avoiding the hard stuff in life. Change becomes harder than ever and we compensate for the stress by exercising behaviors that, though they are unhealthy, serve a clear purpose for us—whether physical, emotional, or psychological.

With some of the experiences we went through in the last couple years, I found myself getting out of my healthy habits for a few weeks, and then I reminded myself of how much better I feel when I do them, so I gave myself grace and got back at it because I know I love how I feel when I am eating healthy and walking a lot.

I'm sure I am not the only one who has found solace in a double scoop of Rocky Road, late at night! It's ok to splurge every once in a while, but night after night is not such a good idea. It will catch up with us.

Are you ready to change your unhealthy habits into healthy ones?

What is your reason? Why do you want to be healthy? Why do you want to take care of yourself? What is your why?

I keep thinking of my family. I want to see my adorable grandbabies grow up, go to school, college, get married one day, and have their own families. I want to be around for that. I love traveling with my husband and usually when we travel, we end up walking miles a day.

I remember when we went to Italy years ago and we averaged walking 10 miles a day. I loved it. We would fall into bed at night, exhausted but it felt great that we could do that.

I had a client years ago whose why was she wanted to get healthy so she could lose weight and be able to get on the floor and play with her grandkids.

So, decide your why, and go for it, friend. Get off the couch, stop making excuses and start doing the healthy habits, one day at a time.

STEPS TO CHANGE UNHEALTHY HABITS

1. *Determine which habits you want to change.* This requires becoming aware of what you are not happy with, not beating yourself up, and then beginning to do the new habits, one at a time.
2. *What are you getting out of your current habit?* Are you numbing life by drinking alcohol every day? Are you seeking comfort in food? Are you always online because it brings a sense of connection? Or binge-watching Netflix into the wee hours of the night because you think you deserve down time? Don't make this step complex, just be aware of this and begin thinking of the positive outcome you will get by changing.
3. *Choose something to replace the negative habit.* So come up with ideas of what you will do when a negative habit arises. If you're standing in front of the refrigerator contemplating eating some more when you are not

even hungry, then plan that you will take a walk, drink more water, and breathe through it. When you do something different to replace an unhealthy habit, acknowledge to yourself that you are doing it differently. You need to bring whatever it is that is subconscious to the conscious mind so that you can recognize your ability to change. It can be as simple as saying to yourself, "Look at that. I made a better choice."

4. *Remove triggers.* If you know that you are always turning to cookies, consider removing them from your home, or only making a few. If drinking too much alcohol is something you need to break, then maybe start by only buying a couple of beers instead of the entire case. Some people need to slowly change their habits, and others can remove the triggers completely. (Remember those barbeque chips I mentioned earlier? I rarely bring those into our house now and recently when we did have some, I put some in a small bowl so I wouldn't eat the entire bag.)

5. *Imagine yourself changing.* If you are wanting to lose weight, find a picture of yourself when you remember feeling really good. Put it on your phone, or your refrigerator, and really think about how you felt then. We are more motivated by feelings. This is an exercise I do with my clients during our sessions.

6. *Be aware of the words you are speaking to yourself.* If you are inclined to tell yourself, "I am so fat," or even "I will never lose weight," I want you to ask yourself, "Have you ever lost weight before?" Yes. So is it true to say never? Reframe those statements too, "Why am I

doing so well on my wellness journey?" or "Why do I love my body?"
7. *Allow yourself to start with baby steps.* If you planned to do an hour workout today and now you can only do 30 minutes, still do the 30 minutes. This will create the habit.
8. *Know it will take time.* It typically takes 21 days to create a habit. It won't be perfect overnight.

As you make better choices and act on various aspects of your life, it is easier to reach your goals. Your good habits will begin to complement and support each other, creating a multiplier effect that will make you see and feel amazing changes in your life.

HEALTHY HABITS THAT HAVE HELPED ME

Be sure and print off this habit tracker:
HabitTracker.DarlaNelson.pdf

Below you will see healthy habits that have been key to helping me with my life and with the stress and anxiety that I have experienced over the years. Most are not in any particular order, except I do believe that habit #1, the one I must do first, is the Habit of Beginning my day with God. When I begin this way, everything else seems to fall into place much easier.

#1 The Habit of Beginning the Day with God

I really think this is one of the most important habits of mine. It's really more than a habit, it's the foundation for everything that follows in my day.

I love the familiar verse in Matthew 6 that says, "But seek first his kingdom and his righteousness, and all these things will be given to you as well."

Life is busy, we are all running here and there, dropping kids off at school, trying to get out the door and be at work by 8:00.

Have you ever woken up and immediately checked your phone, responding to texts, emails, or news? Before you know it, stress and anxiety have taken over, and you're already feeling behind.

We all have distractions in life. We all experience stress and anxiety like I have shared so much with you in this book. But we can start to see ourselves become more calm when we make this habit a priority.

Without grounding in God's peace, small frustrations (spilled coffee, traffic, a snippy comment from a family member) feel overwhelming, and your responses can be from a place of irritation instead of responding from a place of love and grace.

For myself, when I begin my day with some moments of quiet, whether in prayer or just sitting quietly reading scripture, I am able to shift my focus from all the things of self to more of a reliance on God.

Taking time to pray, read Scripture, or worship, even for five minutes with God will help shift your mindset, reminding you that He is in control, not the chaos around you.

On days I don't start with God, I tend to rush into my tasks, and by midday, I feel frazzled and overwhelmed. If something unexpected happens (like a tough conversation or a setback in plans), it's easy to let it dictate my mood.

But on days when I take even a few minutes to read Scripture, pray, or sit in silence with God, I notice a huge difference. I approach the day with more peace, patience, and trust. When challenges come, I'm more likely to say, "Okay, Lord, I trust You in this," instead of spiraling into stress.

It's not about perfection but about preparing our hearts. When we start with God, we invite Him into every moment, and that changes everything. ♡

It strengthens our mindset. We can choose to start our day with anxiety or overwhelm; or start with faith, hope, and confidence in God's plan.

It can really help you to shape your priorities. Instead of being driven by to-do lists and obligations, we can look at our goals from a place with what truly matters—serving, loving, and living with purpose.

#2 The Habit of Drinking Water

Water, water, water. It's amazing how vital this simple liquid is to our health.

It is very common to see me carrying a water bottle everywhere I go.

If you ask me, there's no such thing as too much water; our bodies are thirsty for it, and the benefits are immeasurable. Of course, if you have kidney issues, then a person needs to be careful of their water intake. Just ask your doctor how much you should be drinking in that case.

Did you know that the amount of water you drink each day significantly impacts your overall health?

Staying well-hydrated is crucial because nearly every cell in your body relies on water to function properly. The truth is, our bodies are constantly using water to perform essential tasks like digestion, nutrient absorption, and regulating body temperature.

So, why not give your body the fuel it craves? But how much water should we be consuming daily? Well, a general guideline is to drink half your body weight in ounces of water each day. For instance, if you weigh 150 pounds, that would be 75 ounces of water a day. While this may sound like a lot, trust me, your body craves it. Once you make a habit of drinking water, you'll see it helps with everything from clearer skin to greater energy levels.

Water offers countless health benefits. It replenishes moisture to your organs, helps support healthy digestion, detoxifies, reduces inflammation, and the list goes on!

Simply put, our bodies need water to stay in balance and energized. Imagine replacing sugary drinks or sodas with water—each sip benefits your body in ways soda just can't compare to. In fact, soda, loaded with caffeine and unhealthy sweeteners, causes blood sugar spikes, leading to a rollercoaster of energy crashes that can leave you feeling drained.

What you may not realize is that even "diet" sodas, containing artificial sweeteners like aspartame, are not only linked to headaches but can influence everything from memory and mood to hormones.

Years ago, a friend wanted help on losing weight and she was highly addicted to Diet Coke. Yes, I said Diet Coke. I suggested she started drinking water instead and she gradually weaned herself from Diet Coke. (I say wean, because if you're addicted, you will experience headaches from the lack of caffeine, so don't do it cold turkey.) Guess what happened? She lost weight!! Yes, that is possible.

I always encourage people to make water the primary choice for hydration. I have often run Water Challenges online. Women are amazed how in five days of doing the challenge and paying attention to how much water they are drinking, how much more energy they have.

Some people tell me that water is boring to them. You don't have to settle for plain water. You can infuse it with fresh fruits like lemon, cucumber, or orange slices for that tangy kick. Or even try decaf iced tea for an extra flavor boost!

My favorite decaf drink is an iced tea I make at home all the time. I use four decaf green tea bags and two decaf peach tea bags. I boil them together in a pan, then pour them into a pitcher and add more water. My family loves this tea recipe.

Just remember, caffeinated beverages like coffee and regular tea don't count towards your daily water intake. They might give you a momentary energy lift, but they won't hydrate you the way water will.

I know changing your beverage choices might seem tough at first, but trust me, once this becomes a habit, it will work wonders for your health.

You will take your water bottle everywhere you go, like me. I do love that this seems to be more common these days, to see people carrying water with them.

So, are you ready to make that change? Drink more water, fuel your body properly, and let the transformation of your health begin. Your body will thank you!

#3 The Habit of Choosing Healthy Foods

Changing how I eat has been absolutely crucial for how I feel every day. Over the years, I've taken a variety of nutrition classes learning about digestion, the impact of sugar, and the pitfalls of processed foods. But let me be clear: I'm not a certified nutritionist. I simply learned enough to know what matters for my own health, and I want to share that perspective with you.

You will remember from my story at the beginning of the book, I had to change what I was eating because it was affecting my overall health.

I often hear people ask, "What do I eat?" While that's a great question, knowing what to eat is only half the battle. Because knowledge alone doesn't change behavior. It's about building healthy habits that last.

For example, I remember growing up when convenience was king and microwaves were a new thing! Yes, I am dating myself.

I don't know why this memory stays with me, but my dad came up with an idea to "build in" our microwave in the early 70's. Microwaves were fairly new back then, and people often had this huge microwave just sitting on their countertop. Dad put ours above the oven and framed around it so it looked built in.

My mom bought frozen vegetables because it was simply easier. Growing up in Los Angeles we didn't have a lot of fresh foods nearby. I honestly hated veggies as a kid.

It wasn't until I was married and moved closer to Northern California where we had access to more fresh food and vegetables that I started to really love vegetables. Now I feel I could live on them.

I even recall loving processed foods like boxed macaroni and cheese, Top Ramen, and sugary cereals.

Our kids totally grew up on similar foods as I did. It was totally common to buy cereals ladened in sugar or buy Grape Nuts Cereal and pour on the sugar to make them taste better.

It wasn't until I was inching towards turning 40 that I began to really pay attention because my health was being affected by those unhealthy foods.

Looking back, I realize how much those choices affected me—chronic headaches, constant fatigue, and digestive issues that no one ever linked to what I was eating.

As I began my own journey to health, I learned to let go of the heavily processed foods and focus on whole, natural foods instead. I started shopping along the perimeter of the grocery store—where you find fresh fruits, vegetables, lean meats, and whole grains like quinoa and brown rice. This wasn't just about losing weight; it was about feeling energized, clear-headed, and balanced throughout my day.

I remember a day, sitting at the table with a plate of grilled veggies, so in love with what I was eating, and loving how I was feeling from eating good food. Healthy food. I felt nourished and alive, not just physically, but emotionally as well. It was a simple meal, yet it marked the beginning of a profound shift in my life and how I think about food.

Another important lesson came from reading labels. I learned to avoid foods with long lists of unrecognizable ingredients. I was taught that we should be eating foods that don't have more than 3 ingredients listed. And not to eat foods that the ingredient list starts with a form of sugar.

It's amazing how much sugar is hidden in products we assume are healthy. I even discovered that the average American consumes about 17 teaspoons of added sugar each day! No wonder we experience those energy crashes and persistent headaches.

I also began baking my own Gluten-Free treats: egg cups, blueberry muffins, and more, using natural sweeteners like honey instead of refined sugars. Every small change helped me understand that what we put into our bodies directly affects our energy, mood, and overall health.

There are so many healthy recipes available on Pinterest. And they even help with substitutions if you have certain things you are allergic to.

Let's not forget about fats. I learned the hard way that not all fats are created equal. While our bodies need healthy fats, like Omega-3s from fish and flaxseed, and Omega-6s from nuts and seeds, we should avoid trans-fats that increase bad cholesterol and contribute to inflammation.

Ultimately, the foundation of good health starts with choosing real, whole foods over processed alternatives. It isn't about following every trendy diet; it's about listening to your body and learning what works best for you. Every person is unique; what energizes me might not have the same effect on you, and that's okay.

I share my journey not as an expert, but as someone who has learned from personal experience. I encourage you to explore, ask questions, and discover the habits that will help you thrive. By choosing healthy foods, you're not just feeding your body, you're nurturing your mind and spirit, paving the way for a healthier, happier life.

How to Eat: Slowing Down and Savoring Every Bite

It turns out that how you eat can be just as important as what you eat. So often, we find ourselves rushing through meals, eating on the go, distracted by screens, or simply in a stress response mode. In our busy lives, it's easy to forget that it takes about 20 minutes for your brain to register that you're full. When you eat too quickly, you miss that crucial moment of satisfaction, and before you know it, you've overindulged.

I've struggled with this myself. Even though I try to eat healthy, I have to make a conscious effort to slow down. One of the exercises I do with my clients in my 12-week program is an experiment: we measure how quickly we eat and note when we feel satisfied versus when we tip into overeating. It's eye-opening! A client once told me that learning to eat slower not only improved her digestion and nutrient absorption but also transformed mealtime into a precious opportunity for connection with her family. Dinner became a time when everyone shared the ups and downs of their day, rather than just a hurried break to refuel.

I've also noticed how different environments shape our eating habits. I remember traveling to Italy and experiencing a dinner that lasted nearly four hours. Each course was paired with a perfect glass of wine, and every bite was savored. Although I must admit, I wasn't a fan of some dishes (I still can't stand pigeon!), that slow, deliberate meal was a powerful reminder of how eating slowly can enrich our experience, not just physically, but emotionally and socially, too.

Then there's the challenge of emotional eating. How many times have you found yourself reaching for a bag of chips when you're stressed at work or grabbing dessert even when you're not really hungry? I've been there. Those moments when you know deep down you're not truly hungry, but food seems like the easiest way to soothe your emotions. I used to struggle with this, especially on days when I was juggling work stress and personal challenges. I even had a moment or two, when I was about to order a chocolate lava cake at a restaurant, purely because my emotions were screaming for comfort. Thankfully, I have learned to recognize these triggers.

One tactic that's helped me is to pause and ask myself a series of questions when I am about to reach for food:

- Am I really hungry, or is it just a craving?
- What emotions am I feeling right now—stress, boredom, or sadness?
- Could I satisfy this feeling by taking a short walk, calling a friend, or simply drinking a glass of water instead?

I've also found that being mindful at the table makes a huge difference. I try to put my fork down between bites and take deep breaths, really focusing on the flavors and textures of my food. It might sound simple, but this mindfulness helps me enjoy my meals more and prevents overeating.

For those moments when you catch yourself distracted, such as scrolling through Instagram while eating, I challenge you to try "single-tasking" during meals. Give yourself permission to just be present with your food and the people around you. Over time, this practice can transform not only your eating habits but also your overall well-being. This isn't hard for me when I am eating with others, but when I am eating alone, I often feel I need to be doing something else.

Remember, changing how you eat isn't about following strict rules or diets. It's about building a healthier relationship with food; one that honors your body, respects your hunger signals, and allows you to truly enjoy every bite.

#4 The Habit of Movement: Energizing Your Life Through Exercise

One of the most important components of a healthy lifestyle is exercise. I've learned that making movement a habit can truly transform your life. Over time, I've discovered that exercise isn't just about burning calories or losing weight; it's about energizing your mind, body, and spirit. When I first started on this journey, I experimented with different forms of movement and learned what truly worked for me.

A favorite activity of mine is simply getting out for a walk. I love strolling through nature, listening to the chirping of birds, and even hearing the gentle sound of the local church bells. There's something incredibly peaceful about walking, whether I'm walking alone, where I have time to think, pray, and listen to my favorite podcasts, or walking with a friend, where the conversation and shared experience add another layer of joy. I've come to see walking as much more than physical exercise; it's a form of meditation, a time to reconnect with myself and the world around me.

I know many of you are on a journey to create healthy habits and boost your energy, and exercise is a critical piece of that puzzle. While we've talked a lot about what we eat and how our food choices impact our well-being, exercise offers unique benefits that nutrition alone can't provide. For example, even a simple 30-minute walk, taken consistently, five days a week, can lead to noticeable improvements in your mood, energy levels, and overall health.

Every day when I walk, whether just a mile or three to four miles, I always come home feeling better, more energized and ready to face the day.

You don't need to spend hours at a gym to see results; consistency in small doses is the key.

I still remember a period in my life when I barely set aside time for exercise. I was so caught up in the daily hustle of work, kids' homework, and after-school programs, that I often skipped movement altogether. Then, I realized that if I didn't move, I wouldn't have the energy to handle all those responsibilities. It was a wake-up call: our bodies need movement not only to maintain physical health but also to support mental clarity and emotional resilience. And it's key to take time for you, my friend. It will make you a better mom, wife, friend.

One of the most fun and challenging experiences I've had was when my husband and I decided to do the 8-week Couch to 5K program at the beginning of the pandemic. I have to admit, running has never been my favorite activity, but I was determined to prove to myself that I could do it. Every morning at 5:30 AM, even when it was still dark, we laced up our sneakers and followed an app that gradually increased our running distance. Slowly but surely, we built up to running a full 5K, about 3.1 miles, without stopping. It was fun too, to see others during the pandemic out exercising. I was so proud of that achievement, and it felt even more special because we did it together, cheering each other on. After our run, we would finish with an 8-minute arm workout on YouTube. Although I haven't felt a desire to run since, that experience taught me the value of consistent effort and how small, regular workouts can create lasting change.

Of course, life isn't always about hitting the pavement for a run. I personally have to know what exercises bring joy to me. I have to mix it up to keep things interesting. Last summer, for instance, I made it a point to vary my workouts. Some days I focused on a long walk, averaging about three miles; other days I incorporated yoga or used hand weights for a quick strength session. I learned that variety not only prevents boredom but also challenges different parts of my body, keeping me more engaged and less prone to injury.

I will say though that having a workout plan to follow helps me to have better results.

I have also found as I age, that I have to pay attention to my body and be willing to make adjustments so I don't hurt myself. I used to love doing squats and now I am not able to do them as often or go as low as I could even five years ago, because of the pain I experience in my hip. That can be discouraging, but there are many other exercise moves that I can do instead.

I often hear people say they don't have time to exercise. But have you ever stopped to consider how much time you might be wasting on things that don't serve your health? Perhaps you can spare just 10 minutes here or there, maybe a walk around the block instead of watching another episode of your favorite show. It might sound small, but when you add up those minutes, they create a significant impact. I like to remind myself that energy creates energy. Even on days when I feel low, I know that a short burst of movement can lift my mood and renew my strength.

One memorable example comes from a recent client session. A client of mine had committed to taking a walk after work as a form of self-care. One particularly exhausting day, she nearly skipped her walk because she was so drained. But she pushed through, and the following week, she told me during our client coaching session how that evening walk recharged her so much that she ended up baking a cake and enjoying a relaxed evening with her husband. She realized that even when she felt too tired to move, choosing to exercise actually gave her more energy in return. Her experience is a perfect reminder that sometimes, the act of moving, even when it feels like the last thing you want to do, can break the cycle of exhaustion and stress. And you will be so proud of yourself for doing something for you.

Just this week someone was asking me what type of exercises I do. I then asked her what she does. And she said, "Nothing!" She owns a business, works all day and comes home exhausted, too tired to exercise. But she knows that when she does, she feels better.

What are your excuses? Do you know you feel better when you take at least 15-20 minutes to move? Even just doing some arm exercises feels great.

I've also learned that exercise isn't a one-size-fits-all solution. My personal experience with some arthritis and hypothyroidism has taught me how essential movement is for managing pain and boosting energy. When I miss too many days of exercise, my body starts to ache, I feel stiff, and my energy level is affected. It's almost as if my body is screaming for me to take care of it. That realization pushes me to prioritize regular movement, even on days when I didn't feel up to it. I mix it up to keep my routine interesting, sometimes a brisk walk, other times a gentle yoga session, or even some arm exercises to keep things varied.

Even when time or energy is tight, there are always options. For instance, if you have kids, you might find that dancing around the living room with them or taking a bike ride in the park can be both fun and effective exercise. I've also found that using free online videos is a great way to get a structured workout without the expense of a gym membership. There's an abundance of options out there, each one can be tailored to fit your lifestyle and personal preferences.

One thing I truly believe is that movement not only improves your physical health but also has a profound impact on your mental state. Dr. Hyman has mentioned that exercise boosts metabolism, reduces inflammation, and even lowers the risk of conditions like depression, diabetes, heart disease, and dementia. For me, the most noticeable benefit is the mental clarity and peace it brings. When I feel anxious or overwhelmed, a simple walk often clears my head and helps me regain a sense of calm.

I remember vividly the early days of the pandemic, when my husband and I found ourselves working from home and struggling to maintain our usual routines. Determined not to let the isolation drain our energy, we started a new habit of exercising together. Whether it was following a Couch to 5K program or doing a quick home workout, those shared moments became a cherished part of our day. They not only improved our physical health but also deepened our connection as we supported each other through a challenging time.

Nowadays, we often walk in the evenings after work because it's not just getting our steps in, but it's also a way to catch up on each other's day while we walk.

So, I challenge you to find your own way to incorporate movement into your life. Experiment with different activities until you discover what you truly enjoy. Remember, it doesn't have to be intense or time-consuming, a few minutes of movement each day can create a ripple effect, building energy, strength, and a positive mindset. The key is to start small and be consistent. As you make exercise a habit, you'll begin to notice the energy boost and the improvement in how you feel, both physically and emotionally.

Will you make movement a part of your daily routine? Embrace the habit of exercise and watch as it transforms your energy, your mood, and ultimately, your life.

#5 The Habit of Sleep

Sleep isn't just about shutting down for a few hours, it's a key part of our everyday routine that fuels our physical and mental well-being. Studies show that about one in three adults isn't getting the recommended seven to nine hours of sleep each night, and that lack of rest can affect everything from our mood to our ability to focus.

In fact, research from the CDC suggests that insufficient sleep is linked to higher risks of chronic issues like heart disease and diabetes, not to mention it can seriously sap your energy for the day.

Have you ever struggled with sleep? Waking up often during the night, or having a hard time falling asleep?

I sure have.

I feel I do pretty well falling asleep initially but it's the waking up during the night that causes me to just lay there wide awake, frustrated. I lay there trying to conquer the world, figure everything out, or just worry about all the things that are out of my control.

I am pretty sure God does a lot of work on my heart though in the middle of the night. Nighttime seems to be when I pray the most.

People don't often realize this, but adequate sleep has a lot to do with your overall health and your waistline.

Many effects of a lack of sleep, such as feeling grumpy and not working at your best, are well known. But did you know that sleep deprivation can also have profound consequences on your physical health?

We cannot be sleep deprived for too long before we realize it's influencing our overall health.

Obesity and its associated health problems, such as heart disease and diabetes, can lower your energy level by making you feel fatigued during the day. A poor night of sleep can impact your immune system, making you more susceptible to colds and flus and lowering your energy levels for days at a time.

Have you ever wondered why, when you're sleep deprived, nothing sounds better than some carbs? You reach for the entire sleeve of Ritz Crackers or you down yet another toasted bagel? That is because sleep deprivation actually changes our cravings, turning on this incredible desire for carbs and foods loaded with sugar. When we don't have adequate sleep, our brain will actually struggle to make healthy decisions about how much and what types of food to eat.

Are there certain foods that you notice that if you eat them later in the evening, you will have a miserable night? Do you keep eating them even though you know this? And if so, why?

Evidence suggests that sleep performs a range of vital functions including: restoring damaged tissues, boosting learning and memory, and flushing toxins from the brain.

One in three of us suffer from poor sleep, with stress, computers and taking work home often blamed.

However, the cost of all those sleepless nights is more than just bad moods and a lack of focus.

It's now clear that a solid night's sleep is essential for a long and healthy life.

In today's culture of constant disruption, it's even more important that we create daily habits that will support our well-being. This will allow our minds to be open and receptive to change.

How much sleep do we need?

Most of us need around eight hours of good-quality sleep a night to function properly.

What matters is that you find out how much sleep you need and then try to achieve it.

As a general rule, if you wake up tired and spend the day longing for a chance to have a nap, it's likely that you're not getting enough sleep.

How many of you feel like you lack energy? Are often tired or always tired?

I don't know if you're like me, if I am not getting adequate sleep then the challenges of life can seem so much bigger than they really are.

I used to be tired all the time. As you know from reading my story, growing up with headaches all the time, not knowing what was causing them, I was forever tired. Part of that of course was from not knowing at the time that my thyroid levels were off and I had hypothyroidism. I wonder if my kids remember how much of their young years I was dragging and often would take power naps. I didn't need a two-hour nap or anything, yet a 20 minute one would give me a big boost for the day!

Does this feel familiar to you?

I am amazed now, at how I will go throughout the whole day, the week and realize I never even thought of taking a nap! It's such a great feeling!

There are times though that I can take a nap if I want to, just because I love a good nap and I know my naps are lucky to last more than 20 minutes.

I also notice, like we talked about earlier, on the topic of sugar, that if I eat too much sugar, I am more tired.

Did you know that lack of sleep also boosts your body's production of the stress hormone called cortisol? When cortisol levels are raised, it causes your body to store fat, particularly around your midsection. How many of you wish your midsection was smaller? Could it be that you aren't getting enough sleep?!

A study from researchers in Colorado, found that after only a week of having only five hours a sleep versus the eight that is suggested, participants gained an average of two pounds! The impact of sleep on inflammation, brain health, and weight should not be underestimated.

Sleep deprivation can also make you less likely to be active. Think about it, when you are already tired, the last thing you typically will want to do is head to the gym. The lack of exercise combined with increased cortisol levels can deliver a serious blow to your efforts to live a healthy lifestyle. It's becomes a vicious cycle.

Don't allow a lack of sleep to undermine the healthy lifestyle you have worked so hard to attain. Find a sleep routine that works for you and stick to it. Your body will thank you!!

How can you sleep better?

COMMITTING to not looking at your cell phone right before bed and during the night. I really struggle still with reading on my phone before bed. One thing I am getting better at is if I wake during the night I won't check my phone, scroll FB or Pinterest. That only causes me to become more awake. Instead, I am working on reading a regular paperback book before turning the lights out. It's amazing to me how our bodies will begin to work like clockwork and I wake most days at the same time without an alarm. It's so interesting to me how our bodies get used to waking up at the same time. I don't need an alarm most days unless I have an early morning appointment, because I just automatically wake up now.

According to the national Sleep foundation, 95 percent of people surveyed admitted to using electronic devices prior to sleeping. Researchers have found using these devices so close to bedtime can lead to sleep disturbances, low energy and feeling drowsy the next day.

Here are some more tips for better sleep:

1. Avoid caffeine after noon. This is key for me. I love iced tea and if I have iced tea with caffeine for dinner, it's all over and I will be wide awake for hours.
2. Avoid eating two to three hours before bed. Allow the body to rest, not digest, during the night.
3. Drink decaf drinks, or chamomile, peppermint, or ginger in the evening. I love my decaf iced tea blend I make!
4. Some people find it helpful to use eye masks or earplugs to shut out light and noise.

5. Sleep with your room cooler. This is a big one for me. I prefer to sleep in a cool room even in the winter, so the heater isn't waking me up.
6. Increase your Magnesium. I personally use a product called Natural Calm. Magnesium plays an important role in the functioning of your body and helps reduce the risk of impaired insulin response. Even if you eat a healthy diet, it is very possible that you are not getting enough foods high in magnesium such as dark leafy greens, seeds, nuts, squash, broccoli, meal, dark chocolate. This is why I take magnesium every night before I go to bed.
7. Avoid Alcohol.
8. Avoid sedatives and sleep aids. People's bodies can actually get used to having a Tylenol PM every night.
9. Consider using a white noise app. The one I use is called Relax Melodies. I started doing this a few years ago to help me sleep next to my husband for when he is snoring so I can focus on the sound of ocean waves and not lay there getting irritated with him and the sounds that snoring makes.
10. And exercise. I find that regular exercise helps me to sleep better.

Scientists tell us that a proper sleep cycle involves both REM and non-REM sleep, each playing a crucial role in our physical and mental restoration. I found that when I consistently get a full night's rest, I can think more clearly, handle stress better, and even perform better physically during my workouts. It's no coincidence that many successful individuals stress the importance of sleep as a secret to their high energy and productivity.

Of course, developing a good sleep habit isn't always easy. There are nights when racing thoughts or lingering worries keep me awake. During those times, I've learned to employ practical techniques, like deep breathing exercises, meditating for a few minutes, or simply reading a few pages of a calming book, to gently help my mind slow down and get my body into a restful state.

Think about your own sleep habits: How many hours do you really sleep? Do you find it hard to unwind at night? I invite you to try one new sleep habit this week. Perhaps it's turning off your screens 30 minutes earlier, or maybe it's establishing a pre-bedtime ritual that signals your body it's time to relax. Notice the difference in your mood, energy, and overall well-being.

Quality sleep is a gift you give yourself, a time to rejuvenate and prepare for the challenges and joys of the next day. As you work on building this habit, remember that every small change brings you closer to a more energized, balanced, and joyful life.

#6 HABIT of Intentional Breathing

Intentional breathing is a habit that helps anchor you in the present moment, reducing stress and promoting calm.

Breathing is something we do automatically, but intentional breathing is different. It's a practice of slowing down, focusing on your breath, and using it as a tool to regulate emotions, decrease anxiety, and reconnect with God's presence.

When we're stressed or overwhelmed, our breathing becomes shallow and fast, signaling to the body that we're in danger, even when we're not. This triggers the body's fight-or-flight response, increasing tension and making it harder to think clearly.

But when we breathe intentionally, we activate the body's relaxation response, lowering cortisol (the stress hormone), slowing the heart rate, and creating space for peace. It also allows us to pause and recenter, whether we need to reset our emotions or simply become more aware of God's presence.

Breathing Techniques for Peace & Focus

Here are a few simple, effective breathing techniques to use throughout your day:

1. Box Breathing (The 4-4-4-4 Method)

Perfect for calming the mind and body when feeling anxious or overwhelmed.

How to do it:

1. Inhale through your nose for **4 seconds**.
2. Hold your breath for **4 seconds**.
3. Exhale slowly through your mouth for **4 seconds**.
4. Hold your breath again for **4 seconds**.
5. Repeat the cycle 4-5 times.

Best time to use it: Before a stressful situation, during moments of anxiety, or to reset your focus.

2. 5-5-7 Breathing (The Relaxation Breath)

This technique helps activate the parasympathetic nervous system, which promotes deep relaxation. I love doing this one before my client sessions, so the client and myself are grounded and focused on our time together.

How to do it:

1. Inhale deeply through your nose for **5 seconds**.
2. Hold your breath for **5 seconds**.
3. Exhale slowly through your mouth for **7 seconds**, making a soft whooshing sound.

4. Repeat 3-4 times.

Best time to use it: Before bed, when feeling emotionally overwhelmed, or when needing to recenter in prayer.

3. "Inhale the Good, Exhale the Bad" Breathing.

This technique helps shift your mindset by intentionally breathing in what you need and releasing what no longer serves you. This also is a favorite technique I use with my coaching clients.

1. **Inhale deeply through your nose**, focusing on what you want to receive (peace, joy, love, grace). You can silently say:
2. "I breathe in **peace**."
3. "I breathe in **God's love**."
4. "I breathe in **joy and gratitude**."
5. **Exhale slowly through your mouth**, releasing what you need to let go (stress, fear, frustration, judgment). Silently say:
6. "I breathe out **worry**."
7. "I breathe out **anger**."
8. "I breathe out **self-doubt**."
9. Repeat for **2-5 minutes**, letting the rhythm of your breath align your heart and mind with the shift you're making.

Best times to use this technique:

✔ In the morning to set a positive tone for the day.

✔ During stressful moments to quickly reset your emotions.

✔ Before bed to release the weight of the day and rest in God's peace.

This practice beautifully aligns with Philippians 4:8—focusing on what is good, pure, and lovely—while letting go of what is heavy and harmful.

4. The 5-5-5 Breath (Quick Reset Breath)

A simple way to calm the nervous system in under a minute. How to do it:

1. Inhale through your nose for **5 seconds**.
2. Hold for **5 seconds**.
3. Exhale for **5 seconds**.

Best time to use it: Anytime you feel tension creeping in—before responding to a difficult situation, in traffic, or before an important conversation.

Making Intentional Breathing a Habit

Just like spending time with God, intentional breathing is a small habit that creates big results over time. Consider:

✔ **Starting your day** with deep breathing and a breath prayer.

✔ **Using it in the moment** when stress or frustration arises.

✔ **Ending your day** with a calming breath technique to relax before sleep.

Breath is a gift from God—every inhale and exhale is a reminder that He sustains us. By making intentional breathing a habit, we create space for more peace, clarity, and connection in our daily lives.

#7 The Habit of Financial Awareness: Finding Freedom Through Stewardship

Years ago, we, or I should really say "I" lived in a cycle of spending without thinking, swiping my credit card way too many times, and convincing myself that if I wanted something, I could get it, whether I could afford it or not. Money came in, money went out, and I didn't pay much attention to it all. If something unexpected came up, like a car repair, a medical bill, or a broken appliance, I'd panic and scramble to figure out how to cover it, more often than not, resorting to using a credit card.

I didn't think much about it at the time, but looking back, I realize how much stress and anxiety I put on myself simply by not being financially aware. I thought I was fine. After all, everyone has debt, right? But the reality was, I wasn't fine. I was constantly worried about money, afraid to open bills. I was tired of always having to check our bank accounts to see how much was left.

After the experience we went through in 2008-2010, (you'll remember earlier in the book when I shared our story of going through the down economy and how that influenced my health, too) I knew things had to be different. My husband has never been a spender, he's always been an amazing provider, and if things were going to be better financially, it was going to be because I was going to pay attention and be responsible with our money.

Most people don't realize how much their financial habits affect their mental and emotional well-being. Stress over money is one of the leading causes of anxiety, marital tension, and even health issues. When you aren't in control of your finances, it can feel like you're constantly living in survival mode, always trying to make it to the next paycheck, always worrying about what unexpected expense will pop up next.

But when you become financially aware, when you really start paying attention to where your money is going and make intentional choices, you gain a sense of control, peace, and even empowerment. Just like with nutrition, exercise, sleep, and all the other healthy habits we've talked about, your financial health requires intentionality.

One of the best things I ever did years ago was to start several online savings accounts. Every week I would have $20-25 go into these individual accounts and each account has a purpose. I still do this. And it helped me see how even the smallest amounts of money add up. One of my favorite accounts I started is the 'family travel" fund which we use a few times a year to take our kids and grandkids on trips, so we have quality time together. It feels good because the money has been saved especially for this purpose. It might not seem like $20-25 would account too much and yet it's way more than just about the amount. It's also about the concept of paying yourself first. And let me ask you this, how often do you blow $20 on something you truly don't need and then wish you could go away for a weekend? You can. Just plan for it.

This journey took some time to adjust. To create new habits.

I started small. I didn't overhaul everything overnight, but I made a few key changes that completely transformed the way I view money:

1. **I Created a Spending Plan That Actually Worked for Us**: I prefer the word spending plan to budgets because the word budget sounded restrictive to me. I created a plan of what all our expenses are, from essentials to nonessentials. I even put in money for clothing, getting a manicure, etc., so that I can do those things without feeling guilt. I quickly learned that this helps me feel freedom. When I had a plan for my money, I no longer felt guilty for spending, I knew exactly what I could afford.

2. **I Stopped Emotional Spending**: Just like with emotional eating, I realized I often spent money as a way to make myself feel better. If I was having a bad

day, I'd buy something as a quick pick-me-up. If I was stressed, I'd go shopping just to get out of the house. But once I became aware of this pattern, I learned to pause and ask myself: Do I really need this? Or am I just trying to fill an emotional need with a purchase? One thing I love is flowers and I would go to Costco, want to buy some $14.99 flowers and instead stand in line and transfer the $14.99 to my savings. It wasn't that I didn't have the money, it was that I was choosing not to buy it.

3. **I Paid Off Debt—One Step at a Time**: The mountain of debt felt overwhelming, but I tackled it little by little. I started by paying off the smallest balance first (which gave me a quick win), then rolled those payments into the next debt. Slowly but surely, the weight of debt began to lift. You will remember what I wrote earlier about paying off medical debt that we owed for our daughter's foot surgeries. At first, I would feel irritated every month when paying $1,000's of dollars in medical debt and then I changed my mindset about that, and eventually we got it all paid off.

4. **I Shifted My Mindset to Stewardship**: Instead of seeing money as something to spend, I started seeing it as something to manage well. Everything I have is a blessing from God, and I want to be a good steward of it. This shift in mindset changed everything.

I am so glad I changed my thinking about money. I thought abundance meant having more, when in reality, it's about valuing more. Financial awareness isn't about limitations, it's about choices. It's about stepping into a place of peace and trust instead of stress and overwhelm. It's about shifting from a scarcity mindset ("I can't afford that") to an abundance mindset ("We're choosing to hold off on that right now").

And just like every other area of life, whether it's what we eat, how we move, or how we rest, this is a habit that can be learned and strengthened over time.

So often, financial awareness gets tied to words like budgeting, cutting back, or sacrificing, but I believe in looking at it differently. It's not about not affording something, it's about aligning your resources with what truly brings you joy and fulfillment.

Instead of saying: I can't afford that right now, I started saying: We are choosing to wait on that purchase because we are focusing on something else that's important to us.

Instead of feeling like I had to cut back, I started asking: What do I actually need and value?

Instead of focusing on what I couldn't do, I started focusing on the freedom that came from making empowered decisions.

I still have a ways to go, but I do know, the last 15 years I am grateful I have been way more responsible.

Even this year, my intention is to be more organized with our finances, being more aware of my business deductions, and mileage deductions, not just when taxes are due, but throughout the entire year.

At the core of financial awareness is a simple truth: everything we have is a gift from God. He has entrusted us with resources, and it's up to us to be good stewards of what we've been given.

When I lived unaware, constantly spending without thinking, I wasn't truly trusting God. I was chasing temporary satisfaction instead of long-term peace. But when I began approaching finances with intentionality, I felt a new sense of peace, freedom, and trust in God's provision.

Instead of relying on credit cards, I started relying on God's wisdom.

Instead of spending impulsively, I started making choices that aligned with my values.

And that, my friend, is why this habit has been key to my overall wellness.

Journal Prompts for Reflection & Growth

1. **In what areas of your life have you been living reactively instead of intentionally?** How can you shift your mindset to be more present and purposeful in your daily habits—whether it's in your finances, health, or spiritual walk?
2. **How do you currently view God's provision in your life?** Are there areas where you need to trust Him more, whether in your finances, health, or personal growth?
3. **Think about your daily habits—what small choices are you making that either support or hinder your well-being?** Are you drinking enough water, nourishing your body with healthy foods, getting enough rest, and moving your body regularly? What is one small step you can take today to improve in one of these areas?
4. **What does abundance mean to you?** Does your current lifestyle, your choices, routines, and mindset, align with that definition? If not, what changes can you begin to make to create a life that reflects true abundance in health, faith, relationships, and finances?

mindset ("I can't afford that") to an abundance mindset ("We're choosing to hold off on that right now").

And just like every other area of life, whether it's what we eat, how we move, or how we rest, this is a habit that can be learned and strengthened over time.

So often, financial awareness gets tied to words like budgeting, cutting back, or sacrificing, but I believe in looking at it differently. It's not about not affording something, it's about aligning your resources with what truly brings you joy and fulfillment.

Instead of saying: I can't afford that right now, I started saying: We are choosing to wait on that purchase because we are focusing on something else that's important to us.

Instead of feeling like I had to cut back, I started asking: What do I actually need and value?

Instead of focusing on what I couldn't do, I started focusing on the freedom that came from making empowered decisions.

I still have a ways to go, but I do know, the last 15 years I am grateful I have been way more responsible.

Even this year, my intention is to be more organized with our finances, being more aware of my business deductions, and mileage deductions, not just when taxes are due, but throughout the entire year.

At the core of financial awareness is a simple truth: everything we have is a gift from God. He has entrusted us with resources, and it's up to us to be good stewards of what we've been given.

When I lived unaware, constantly spending without thinking, I wasn't truly trusting God. I was chasing temporary satisfaction instead of long-term peace. But when I began approaching finances with intentionality, I felt a new sense of peace, freedom, and trust in God's provision.

Instead of relying on credit cards, I started relying on God's wisdom.

Instead of spending impulsively, I started making choices that aligned with my values.

And that, my friend, is why this habit has been key to my overall wellness.

JOURNAL PROMPTS FOR REFLECTION & Growth

1. **In what areas of your life have you been living reactively instead of intentionally?** How can you shift your mindset to be more present and purposeful in your daily habits—whether it's in your finances, health, or spiritual walk?
2. **How do you currently view God's provision in your life?** Are there areas where you need to trust Him more, whether in your finances, health, or personal growth?
3. **Think about your daily habits—what small choices are you making that either support or hinder your well-being?** Are you drinking enough water, nourishing your body with healthy foods, getting enough rest, and moving your body regularly? What is one small step you can take today to improve in one of these areas?
4. **What does abundance mean to you?** Does your current lifestyle, your choices, routines, and mindset, align with that definition? If not, what changes can you begin to make to create a life that reflects true abundance in health, faith, relationships, and finances?

AFTERWORD
YOUR JOURNEY BEGINS NOW

"Do not conform to the pattern of this world, but be transformed by the renewing of your mind." (Rom. 12:2 NIV)

As I sit here, wrapping up this book, I find myself reflecting on the journey we've taken together. From the power of words to the weight of stress, from unpacking emotional burdens to trusting God in the unknown, and finally, to the daily habits that shape our lives—this book has been a collection of lessons, stories, and truths that I have lived, learned, and continue to embrace. I have laughed and I have cried as I wrote. Some days I had no words and others I couldn't type fast enough, all in hopes that my story, my life, my experiences would impact yours.

I wrote this book out of a sincere desire to help you. It will give me great joy to know that this book has impacted your heart. I have absolute confidence and belief in the learnings and scripture that I have shared in this book. They work, when worked.

But now, the question is, what will you do with all of this?

AFTERWORD

How often do we read books, feel inspired, and then set them aside, never applying what we've learned? I don't want this to be just another book you read and forget. My hope is that it has impacted you, challenged you, and caused you to think about your own life in a deeper way.

YOUR MINDSET IS THE FOUNDATION OF EVERYTHING

If there is one message that echoes through every chapter of this book, it's this: Your mindset affects everything.

- The way you speak about yourself and others determines the direction of your relationships.
- The way you think about stress determines whether it controls you or empowers you.
- The way you process grief determines whether you stay stuck in sorrow or move forward in healing.
- The way you approach trust determines whether you live in peace or struggle for control.
- The way you view your habits, whether it's what you eat, how you move, how you spend, or how you rest, determines the quality of your life.
- And ultimately, the way you view God determines the peace, joy, and purpose you will experience.

Your mindset shapes your entire life. The thoughts you allow to take root in your heart will bear fruit, either good or bad. This is why God calls us to renew our minds. It's not about simply changing one habit here or there; it's about transforming the way you think so that the life you desire flows naturally from that change.

TRANSFORMATION BEGINS WITH ONE STEP

You don't have to overhaul your life in one day. Change doesn't happen overnight, and it certainly doesn't happen by striving in your own strength. True, lasting transformation happens when you align your mindset with God's truth and take one step at a time.

- **Want to change your health?** Start with your next meal. Choose to nourish your body instead of just feeding it.
- **Want to change your finances?** Start with your next purchase. Ask yourself, "Does this align with the abundant life I want to create?"
- **Want to change your energy levels?** Start with your next decision to move your body. Go for a walk. Stretch. Do something that reminds you of the strength you have.
- **Want to change your relationship with God?** Start with your next quiet moment. Pause. Pray. Let Him meet you right where you are.

YOU ARE IN CONTROL OF THE CHOICES YOU MAKE

No one else can do this for you. No one else can shift your mindset, build your habits, or strengthen your faith. You have been given the gift of choice. Every day, you are either moving closer to the life you desire or further away from it.

So, here's my challenge to you:

Don't let this book be just another book you read and shelve. Let it be the catalyst for real change in your life. Choose one thing

—just one—that stood out to you and commit to taking action on it today.

Maybe it's drinking more water. Maybe it's speaking kinder words over yourself. Maybe it's learning to let go of something weighing you down. Maybe it's choosing trust over control. Whatever it is, take that first step. And then another.

THIS IS YOUR LIFE. LIVE IT INTENTIONALLY.

You were never meant to live a life of stress, exhaustion, or regret. God has called you to a life of peace, abundance, and purpose. But it starts with your mindset, your choices, and your willingness to take action.

So, my friend, as you close this book, I want you to ask yourself:

- **What will I do differently today because of what I've learned?**
- **What mindset shift do I need to make to align my life with God's truth?**
- **What small habit can I commit to today that will lead to long-term transformation?**

I believe in you. I believe in the work that God is doing in your life. And I pray that this book has been more than just words on a page, a turning point in your journey toward a healthier, more abundant, and more joyful life.

Now go. Live it. Embrace it. And never stop growing.

And P. S. I love you.

WHAT'S NEXT

What's Next?

Your journey doesn't stop here…

If *I'm Fine. Really?* stirred something in your heart, I'd love to stay connected and walk alongside you as you take your next steps toward peace, purpose, and joy.

Here's how we can stay in touch:

📱 Follow me on Instagram for encouragement, daily mindset tips, and faith-based support: @coachdarlanelson

🌐 Visit my website for free resources, coaching opportunities, and upcoming events: www.coachdarlanelson.com

💜 Join my email community and get access to tools like *The Weight Behind I'm Fine*, my free eBook for women seeking more calm and clarity.

📝 Book a complimentary discovery call if you're ready to explore life coaching and create lasting, meaningful change—mentally, physically, and spiritually.

You were never meant to carry the weight of "fine" alone. Let's move forward—together.

A NOTE FROM DARLA

If *I'm Fine. Really?* spoke to your heart, encouraged you, or helped you, would you consider leaving a review?

Your words matter more than you know—not just to me, but to someone else who may be searching for hope, peace, or a reminder that they're not alone.

Your honest review helps this message reach the people who need it most.

Thank you for reading, for caring, and for walking this journey with me.

With gratitude and grace,

Darla

BIBLIOGRAPHY

Books I referred to:

1. *Switch On Your Brain: The Key to Peak Happiness, Thinking, and Health.* Dr. Caroline Leaf. Baker Publishing Group, Michigan. 2013
2. *Afformations: The Miracle of Positive Self Talk.* Noah St. John. Hay House. 2013
3. *The Power of Positive Thinking.* Norman Vincent Peale. Prentice Hall. 1956
4. *The Power of One More: The Ultimate Guide to Happiness and Success.* Wiley. 2022
5. *The Mountain is You-Transforming Self Sabotage into Self Mastery.* Thought Catalog Books. 2020
6. *MONEY: A Love Story-Untangle Your Life Woes and Create the Life You Really Want.* Hay House. 2013

Songs:

Truth Be Told. Mathew West and Carly Pearce. 2021.

ACKNOWLEDGMENTS

To the guy who always stands by my side—my husband, Larry Nelson.

Your unwavering support has been my strength. In the moments when I wanted to give up, you lifted me up. In my coaching journey, you have believed in me even when I doubted myself, always encouraging my passion for helping others. Most of all, you have loved me just as I am.

We make an amazing team, with the help of God, and I cherish every moment we share. I love you more than words can ever express.

To My Dear Daughter, Brooke

Life has a way of teaching us through the people we love most, and you, my sweet Brooke, have been one of my greatest teachers. Watching you walk through some hard experiences challenged me in ways I never expected, stretching my heart and deepening my trust in God. Through it all, He has been faithful, and I have seen His strength in both of us.

Now, not only are you my daughter, but you are also my dearest friend. Your unwavering support in my life and business means more than I can say. When doubt creeps in, you remind me to turn back to God—the One who has always been our foundation.

I am forever grateful for you and the bond we share. I love you more than words can express.

To My Dear Sons, Jake and Kyle

Being your mom has been one of the greatest blessings of my life. Watching you grow into the incredible men, husbands, and fathers you are today fills my heart with gratitude. Walking alongside you as you navigate life - your choices, your relationships, and your own journey of fatherhood - has been a gift beyond measure.

Your dedication, strong work ethic, and commitment to your businesses inspire me daily. You have built lives rooted in integrity, perseverance, and faith, and I couldn't be prouder of the men you have become. Through every challenge and success, I have seen God's hand guiding you, and I trust He will continue to lead you in all that you do.

No matter where life takes you, my love and prayers will always be with you.

I love you more than words can express.

ABOUT THE AUTHOR

Darla Nelson has been married to her husband for 38 years, and together they have built a life filled with love, faith, and family. She is a proud mother of three adult children, all married, and a joyful grandmother to five wonderful grandchildren. Family is her greatest blessing.

As a Christian life coach, Darla has a heart for helping women (and a few wise men) overcome stress, anxiety, and relationship struggles by embracing God's peace and purpose. Her deep faith and personal experiences have inspired her to write this book, offering encouragement, biblical wisdom, and practical tools to help men and women navigate life's challenges.

Her passion is to remind men and women that no matter what they are facing—whether it's grief, self-doubt, or the weight of daily pressures—God is present, offering guidance and hope. Through storytelling and biblical truths, she invites readers to shift their mindset, strengthen their relationships, and find joy in the journey.

When she's not coaching, writing, or spending time with her family, you can find Darla enjoying quiet moments with God, or reading a good book. She also loves spending time outdoors, walking in nature, and sharing laughter and good conversation with her girlfriends at her favorite local restaurants.

Stay connected with Darla at **www.coachdarlanelson.com** or follow her on social media:

- **Instagram:** @coachdarlanelson
- **Facebook:** @coachdarlanelson

www.ingramcontent.com/pod-product-compliance
Lightning Source LLC
Chambersburg PA
CBHW030520080526
44586CB00011B/261